Potholes
in the
Pavement

Inspiring Tales of Vulnerable Children

Marilyn Siden

Copyright © 2017 by Marilyn Siden

Potholes in the Pavement
Inspiring Tales of Vulnerable Children
by Marilyn Siden

Printed in the United States of America.

ISBN 9781545601587

All rights reserved solely by the author. The author guarantees all contents are original and do not infringe upon the legal rights of any other person or work. No part of this book may be reproduced in any form without the permission of the author. The views expressed in this book are not necessarily those of the publisher.

Unless otherwise indicated, Scripture quotations taken from The Message (MSG). Copyright © 1993, 1994, 1995, 1996, 2000, 2001, 2002. Used by permission of NavPress Publishing Group. Used by permission. All rights reserved.

www.xulonpress.com

"Sometimes I would like to ask God why He allowed poverty, suffering and injustice when He could do something about it."

"Well, why don't you ask Him?"

"Because I am afraid He would ask me the same question."

Abdu'l-Baha

DEDICATION

Potholes in the Pavement is dedicated to thousands of children who changed my life and taught amazingly important lessons about Hope and Perseverance and how to live life to the max.

Acknowledgements

It would take volumes to list all the people who have been instrumental in bringing *Potholes in the Pavement* to print.

Xulon Press has served as a constant encouragement since we first discussed the possibility of such an endeavor. They sent me to an amazing young woman, Erika Bennett. She painstakingly poured over every word and corrected more errors than should be legal. And she did it with love and a pretty good sense of humor.

My four remarkable children and their spouses would not let me quit when inspiration faltered, and I did not know where to go next. I am particularly grateful that throughout our Wilderness Trails and Today's Youth Matter journey together, they have all worked in the ministry to further God's Kingdom with hurting young people.

My husband, Doug, never faltered in his support, even when ideas for a chapter came in the middle of the night.

And from the start, my remarkable Savior walked alongside the entire journey. We have had countless conversations on long walks through Alameda. I felt His loving Hand every step of the way.

DISCLAIMER

The names of the children that have touched my life in *Potholes in the Pavement* have been changed for their protection. Some of the story details have been altered to protect children living in unusual circumstances.

TABLE OF CONTENTS

Introduction... xiii
Potholes in the Pavement 19
Lisa 23
Are You Jesus? 26
Janice.. 30
The Grasshopper...................................... 38
The Nursing Home Pig 44
Jamal... 52
Karate and Jesus 60
Eric 63
Not the Hill 69
In a Whisper 74
Asleep on the Trail 77
The Baseball Cap 81
Today's Adults Matter................................ 86
Lost 90
Pull Ups.. 96
The Box Under the Bed 100
Uganda Part One..................................... 106
Uganda Part Two..................................... 116
Brandi 122

Mud in Your Face 125
It Pays to Keep Promises 127
Sally Salamander 133
Lizardbeth....................................136
I Got Your Back 138
Touch that Dial 144
When Good Enough Isn't........................151
Donkeys 156
I'm Just Praying for Forgiveness 165
Forty Feet of Sheer Heaven 170
And Now, the Rest of the Story 174
Memories 178
It is Better to Have Friends.......................186
The Picnic Basket 190
Your Own Personal Rooting Section 196
Cold Cereal...................................200
Cynthia 204
A Home of Our Own...........................209
Science Camp 215
Giving and Giving and Giving 220
Seven Pair of Underwear 223
I've Got Him..................................228
Horse Camp 233
Tony 238
The Anatomy of a Volunteer......................242
Forty-Four Suggestions to Get Started 246
A Final Note 255

INTRODUCTION

Most of my younger years were spent trying to find any avenue for service, as long as it was very public, and I would be seen in an extremely positive light – without the effort of actually doing anything of significance. Doing what I wanted when I wanted and how I wanted seemed the practical and natural way to go. Any effort toward doing something that might positively influence the lives of others had to have an obvious, tangible payoff. One year it was saving the whales. Another year it was the endangered salt marsh mouse. Eventually, I graduated to what, at the time, seemed to be a *higher calling*. I joined Another Mother for Peace and protested wars all over the world. Then it was hungry children, and all environmental issues. Still the pursuit of chasing after *good* and *valuable* but quite distant ideals left me feeling empty and not very useful.

In addition to a variety of causes, I looked to find spiritual truth and dabbled in everything imaginable. It is part of our very being to recognize we all have the heart-shaped empty so many great theologians have written about. And so, my search to seek the truth about me led to dabbling in a little Buddhism, a group called Creative Initiative, and even Erhard Seminar Training. Empty, empty and still empty.

Of course, I had rejected Christianity when I entered and completed college. After all, I was a University of California Berkeley graduate (with a GPA of 2.000001) and therefore could think with the most brilliant minds on the planet. I certainly did not need the crutch of Jesus with the promise that He would save me today and for eternity. At the time, that made no sense.

Then, an acquaintance invited me to come to a puppet show at his church with, "I think your kids will love it." On that day in May 1980, I was introduced to Jesus, who promised to walk alongside me and bring peace to my scattered life. I don't remember much about that day except all the tears and a huge sense of peace that was extremely overwhelming.

One of the first verses I memorized was from Psalm 37:4: "Delight yourself in the Lord, and He will give you the desires of your heart." *(NIV)* It was *beyond* unbelievable. I delight and trust in God and then I get to do whatever I want to do? For those of you walking with God for many years, I am sure you might be smiling at my naïve earliest translation of that simple, yet complex, verse. As with so many new believers, I expected things to change quickly. And part of it did for me. Within a few short weeks, I began my adventure working with children who were enduring unbelievable abuse and neglect. It has been my deep joy to continue this work for a little over thirty-six years.

Introduction

Deciding to let go of so much that defined my life, to that point, was another story. I wish I could claim the path I was on completely changed in my earliest Christ-following years. It was a long and painful process to see my surroundings through eyes other than my own myopic pair. Sadly, it still is going on to this day. Experience slowly pointed me in a new direction that serving others is not only the right thing to do; it is the only thing that has lasting staying power and deep satisfaction. After years of serving, with me at the center of the universe, Christ introduced me to the power of downward mobility. It is a concept most of us miss in a world where top dog is what we strive for. As small children, we play "King of the Mountain," and the fastest to the table gets the best of whatever is served. Downward mobility is rarely seen as a virtue – unless occasionally you strive to be a Mother Teresa type – at least for a season.

The Bottom of the Ladder never seemed to catch on. When I hear words like, "I think what you are doing is great, but I could never be a part of that," it only adds fuel to my self-centered nature to present the best me to those who wonder what downward mobility might really look like. Since I would most likely never have the skills to be a Bill Gates, or have a Dolly Parton voice this seemed like a good alternative. The idea of turning toward serving others with their best interest in mind seemed worth giving a try. I could never have predicted the outcome. Slowly, way too slowly, it began to change me in the process.

I experienced a nine-year stint with Wilderness Trails, a southern Oregon ministry. Then I moved to California, and with a whole lot of tender people looking to reach out to help hurting kids, Today's Youth Matter was born in 1990.

My tendency, when working with battered children is to want to be the giver. Always. Let the kids be on the receiving end for a change. With everything they have endured, through no fault of their own, is that not the right thing to do? The answer is a resounding YES – and NO.

Simply giving to children is a huge mistake. Not only does it prevent the joy of service, but it also forces them to remain amongst the walking wounded.

If we truly want to see children – physically battered and vulnerable or completely loved and cared for – grow into healthy adults, they must learn at an early age the lesson of the master servant, Jesus. Read Philippians 2, and even the densest amongst us are pointed in a new direction:

> Think of yourselves the way Christ Jesus thought of himself. He had equal status with God but didn't think so much of himself that he had to cling to the advantages of that status no matter what. Not at all. When the time came, he set aside the privileges of deity and took on the status of a slave, became human! Having become human, he stayed human. It was an incredibly humbling process. He didn't claim special privileges. Instead, he lived a selfless, obedient life and then died a selfless, obedient

death – and the worst kind of death of all: a crucifixion.

Becoming more and more like Jesus means becoming more and more servant like. Most of us already know that. We just have to take that first step to get out of our own way and do something.

Potholes in the Pavement tells the stories of young survivors and those struggling with life on a day-to-day basis. This book is written for those in the process of deciding to make a difference and turn the tide in the life of a child (or family) falling between the cracks right in front of us. We have a chance to stand alongside and become the hands and feet of the Great Physician and Healer. This may set you on a new course, one guaranteed to bless you beyond your wildest expectations.

POTHOLES IN THE PAVEMENT

Potholes in the pavement. Sometimes they are annoying – sometimes actually quite dangerous. It's difficult to accept them as part of the hazard of my already pretty hazardous daily commute. I recently talked to an engineer from a county roads' department and asked what seemed to be a simple enough question. "What causes potholes in the pavement?"

We were at a social gathering, not the best time to pose such a question. He politely tried to explain in single-syllable laymen's language. "Well, it's almost never just one thing. Sometimes forces from the outside like lots of heavy trucks or prolonged rain pound the road and break it up. Sometimes it's the freezing cold followed by extreme heat. Or there may be a weak spot under the pavement from an unexpected subterraneous – sorry – underground water source. When pressure comes from above or below, the road collapses."

That sounded pretty basic, so I pressed for a little more. "But why does the pothole appear in one part of the road and not another, even though the same trucks or flood waters effect the whole road – not to mention hot and cold weather conditions?"

I guess he thought his pothole explanation had gone far enough, so with just a hint of sarcasm he repeated, "It is never just one thing all by itself. If it were that simple and that easy to predict where a pothole might develop, wouldn't we stop it before it started?"

That is the real question that begs for a plausible answer. Not about roads and not-so-predictable potholes, but about our children. Can we stop the inevitable from happening to our vulnerable kids? Children living in an unspeakably abusive environment develop the beginnings of potholes long before anyone might notice a possible weak spot. They – like potholes in the pavement – begin to crumble when inner and outer forces press in on them. More often than not, it goes unnoticed by teachers, by peers, by church leaders and even by case workers trained to identify sensitive areas that will eventually collapse with even the slightest pressure.

Left to their own devices, children find a way to maneuver through life despite these dangerous potholes. They join a gang for protection and a sense of family when they feel vulnerable, and they are forced to pay a horrific price. The lure of alcohol and drugs offer instant relief, again at a price. Even prostitution, pimping and drug dealing provide a sense of identity and belonging. All vulnerable children are looking for the same thing – a sense of permanence. They are willing to do whatever it takes to find it.

After thinking it over, and not having the courage to track down the same engineer for a little more in-depth insight to this whole pothole analogy, I decided to go to another source of information. A friend with a really bright kid who was working in the field of engineering was willing to dumb down a bit for my beginner perspective. He cordially responded:

A road is first constructed with a solid base material (usually aggregate base) and then new pavement is placed upon the base either asphalt concrete (asphalt) or Portland Cement Concrete. Potholes usually occur in asphalt. Over time the new pavement begins to weather and become more brittle and with regular vehicle loads hairline cracks start to form. These cracks left untreated will grow, so routine preventive maintenance such as crack sealing and minor repairs need to be performed to help slow down this process and extend the life of pavement. Left untreated the cracks grow until water and loading from vehicles begins to break up the pavement, and then a pothole forms. The areas then grow into larger repairs, which can then require removing a larger section of asphalt down to the base material, re-compacting the base and then placing new asphalt. A pothole and roadway are a lot like a house; routine preventive maintenance like painting prevents those deeper and more costly repairs such as repair dry rot and eventually replacement of structural wood framing.[1]

Most vulnerable children do not begin life with that "solid base material." Their world often begins with chaos, violence, and weak spots everywhere. Trying to build anything that will withstand the barrage that life inevitably will bring simply does not work very well with a porous shaky foundation. But this is exactly what they need! A foundation that can withstand anything when life turns south. Then occasional repair and maintenance work is possible. And for vulnerable youngsters (and perhaps for all of us), the only solution is to walk with the One able to offer a new permanent, solid foundation. It becomes our job – our joy – to be the hands and feet of God during a child's entire healing process.

If our society has any desire to prevent the inevitable, we must do something now. It will certainly require hard work, long hours and a mindset of never giving up. It will take more than a little effort to help fractured families build solid permanent foundations that will not crumble under pressure.

LISA

Lisa sat quietly on our drive back to her apartment complex. She nervously glanced over several times, and finally asked, "Are you sometimes afraid to drive me home?"

Lisa lives in a dilapidated apartment building located in a drug-infested neighborhood with all the trappings of drive by shootings and drug deals. Graffiti covers the outside of her building, spilling across the parking lot to the overflowing garbage dumpsters. She sometimes wakes up staring into the red eyes of one of the rats living somewhere in the complex.

She moves awkwardly when she is outside her neighborhood. Lisa knows she does not fit in. Her dreams of designer jeans and that pretty blouse she saw in the window of a local department store are way out of her financial reach. Lisa rationalizes they probably do not have it in her size anyway. She is overweight and out-of-shape. Exercising regularly is something her neighborhood never does. As the day winds down, residents retreat behind barred windows and triple locked doors.

The United States is loaded with untouchable areas. We call them ghettos, the lower bottom, the hood, and the other side of the tracks. They have the reputation of too many gangs, guns, inevitable gunfire and dysfunctional families.

Vulnerable children and their less than perfect families are all around us. They cause me to lock my car doors if I am stopped at a red light, and they are heading in my direction. They make me nervous at night and sometimes even in the daytime.

It is hard to admit that we cannot always predict when tough kids will invade our space. In a perfect world we could. Then we would be able to build our fortress long before they showed up. Then we would never have to deal with all that unpredictability. Unfortunately, they are not the only kids wearing oversized jeans, undoubtedly hiding something up to no good. Some arrive at school with dirty wrinkled clothes and week-old, urine-soaked underwear. Sometimes they fade into the walls behind them; sometimes they are tough – the school bully – but the results are the same. Classmates leave them alone.

We forget, at one time they were children with promise; they were good readers in the second grade, could sing with the best and had all the potential of a great athlete in the making. Their hopes and dreams had no chance to flourish with a drug-addicted mother at home, a father in prison, an abusive uncle or exposure to an R-rated life.

It is too easy to believe that these kids have nothing to do with me. If I just don't go to "that part of town," I can live my life without rocking the boat. Edith Kelly summed it up when she wrote, "The further you are from the frontlines, the more you think everything is okay."[2] Ask any person in the military. It is hard work and way too dangerous on the frontline.

The cost of doing nothing with a whole population of vulnerable children is substantial – perhaps more than anyone wants to admit. As children fall deeper and deeper into despair and the gangs, violence and dysfunction that surrounds them, the likelihood of a life of crime and eventual lock-up skyrocket. Juvenile Hall costs all of us from $30,000 to $148,000[3] each year per youngster (depending upon where you live). Adult prison is a little less. You and I do a much better job caring for high-risk, vulnerable children with our love, at a lot less expense, than the juvenile justice system does with lock up.

Zig Ziglar once commented that if we do not do something soon, those very children will grow up and bring us all down by the sheer weight of them. We can do something now at far less expense.

Underneath that tough exterior lies a child waiting for someone to come alongside and lead them in a different direction. They are seeking role models, friends, someone to love and love them back and perhaps a little laughter – all missing ingredients in their community.

Potholes in the Pavement is the stories of young survivors and those struggling with life on a day-to-day basis.

This book is written for those in the process of deciding to make a difference and turn the tide in the life of a child (or family) falling between the cracks right in front of us.

Are You Jesus?

Eight-year-old identical twin girls—I met at them at camp and instantly we became friends. It would take more than two years before I could identify them correctly by name – 80% of the time!

They entered my life permanently about one year later. Today's Youth Matter (TYM) was forming a Princess Club (after all, we *are* daughters of the King), and because they lived so close to my home – an easy drive for me – I invited them to join our new club. We would meet at least twice a month, and all activities were decided by a group vote. We never made it to an art exhibit, but we visited a number of amusement parks and ate way too many pizzas.

About two years after joining the Princess Club, I took the two of them along with one other from the Club to live on a farm in Oregon for a week. We rode horses and collected chicken eggs. To be expected, egg collecting was a completely new activity. One of the twins proclaimed, "Oh, *that's* where eggs come from! I just thought they came from the store." We picked vegetables— eating some and giving the rest away to homeless folks in a nearby city. They were all pretty surprised potatoes actually grew under the ground!

On Sunday, I took the girls to a very small church about a half-mile from the farm. Our three TYM girls made up 75% of their Sunday school class, and the teacher, when she learned we were coming, went to great lengths to make sure the girls felt welcome. While they were in their class, I joined the adult class of fourteen or so – a good part of the entire congregation. What we studied that morning, I cannot remember. The events during and after the class will remain with me forever.

About half way through my class, a man – perhaps in his early to mid-fifties – joined our small group. Because of the large windows in our classroom, we could see him coming. Judging from the uncomfortable expression on everyone's faces, he had been here before. He rode up on an old, rusty, one-speed bicycle that was pulling a small lopsided cart. All his earthly possessions were stacked up in that cart, and as he came to a stop in front of the church, he retied the string holding things in place to make sure everything remained secure. His long, flowing white gown reminded me of something out of our Lord's era, and he straightened the sash that tucked his gown high enough to keep it from catching in the bicycle chain. Now it almost touched the ground. His full beard and long hair spilled over kind eyes and a soft smile. He certainly would have better fit in the Haight-Ashbury scene in San Francisco than in this rural community where his dress was definitely not the norm.

"He's homeless. Most likely a war vet. His mind is – you know – pretty well gone." In a harsh whisper, the woman sitting next to me started to give me a running account of his history as only she knew and definitely wanted to share, when he walked into the room. No one moved to make room for him around the table. No one even made eye contact with him. He walked slowly to a leftover pew bench in the corner, slipped off his sandals and sat down quietly. He must have known the drill. He was welcome to listen, but he most definitely was not a member of this church.

When the Sunday school class ended, the girls came bounding into the room eager to show me the wonderful things they made and the stories that related to them. There was some beautiful colorful artwork that matched the valuable lesson they learned about following Jesus.

Almost immediately, they spied the overflowing plate of cookies, a giant sheet cake and unlimited hot chocolate packages. My nod of approval needed no additional prompting. They forged to the front of the line to load up on all the goodies.

It was at that moment they saw the "homeless war casualty." All three left their sacred spot in line and slowly approached him. Two girls immediately sat at his feet, and the other asked if he wanted something to eat. He nodded, and she went to bring back cookies, cake and the thickest hot chocolate she could make – several packages of the mix in one small Styrofoam cup. Actually, it was almost a paste, but I knew she was trying to impress him with cocoa just the way she liked it. Then, as if gathering up all the nerve needed to present such an amazingly outlandish question, one of the girls asked, "Are you Jesus?"

He smiled slightly, a genuine joy showing through twinkling eyes and replied, "No." One of the twins looked at me for a better answer. She came over and whispered in my ear, "We asked him if he was Jesus, and he said he wasn't, but I think he is." Until we left the church, the girls kept bringing more food, watching him intently for any telltale signs he was in fact who they were sure he was.

We have the possibility of facing our Lord in the most unexpected places and under the most unlikely circumstances. God came near, and three precious young ladies did not miss the opportunity. They saw what I missed. As we drove away, the words of our Lord kept ringing in my ears, "I was hungry and you fed me. I was thirsty and you gave me something to drink." (Matthew 25:35)

JANICE

Even before our group of twenty started the weeklong backpacking trek into the mountains, it started to rain. And it never stopped. That made absolutely no difference to Janice. We all knew before we even left the parking lot she was way out of her element – her mascara smudging in long streaks down her cheeks because of the rain and her bright red slightly off center lipstick were a dead give-away. She threw herself into that trip in a way rarely seen in teenage girls from any background.

Janice was short – barely five feet tall. She was also considerably overweight. Transferring all her belongings from her suitcase to a backpack, there was no talking her out of extra pants, a clean shirt for every day, several pair of shoes, her makeup kit and even her oversized boom box. (I-pods or even CD players wouldn't come on the market for at least another ten years. Ah, for the not-so-good old days!) It required eight size D batteries (plus a spare eight, just in case), and there was virtually no room in her backpack for anything but her music maker! After tying all her belongings to the various parts of the pack and realizing it wouldn't work in the rain, she devised a "raincoat" for the boom box so she could carry it and stuffed everything else into her backpack. She was ready to go.

Janice told me two things about herself within the first quarter mile of our first day hiking. She was the second toughest girl in her high school, and she loved to sing.

When quizzed about her status as number two in school, she went into a long dissertation about "Numero Uno" as she put it. "She's tough. She's really tough. If you don't want to end up in the hospital, don't mess with her. I just pretend to be tough. I've got all the moves, so people just leave me alone."

Then she laughed. "There was that time when one of the jocks at school told me I was fat – in front of a whole bunch of kids. It really pissed me off. I got to school early the next morning with a fish from our freezer. I waited until I saw him drive into the parking lot, and when he and his jock friends got out and went into school, I popped off one of his hubcaps and put the fish inside. A few days later, it was the talk of the school. No one would even consider riding with him. I don't think he ever figured out why his car stunk so bad!"

Watching Janice walk along the trail was actually quite comical. Backpack completely full. Pillow attached to the top – in the rain. Shoes (two pair) dangling from their shoelaces on the side of the pack – also in the rain. And the boom box in her hand with its little raingear. She could have been the main attraction from a local circus.

The first night, we rigged up some fairly dry lean-tos. The girls slipped into their sleeping bags begging for us to serve dinner in bed. It had taken a good hour to get a fire started, and there was a sense that if the rain didn't stop soon, we might have to pray for Noah to show up. We honored their request with a simple meal of hamburgers, hot chocolate and rather damp cookies. It suited them just fine, and several went to sleep almost immediately.

Not Janice. She was bone tired, but she wanted to sing. That was our first introduction to what might have become the American Idol of the century! Her voice soared above the towering trees surrounding us. It was crystal clear, powerful, but with a distinct soft quality that kept the requests coming well into the night. When the sky briefly cleared, the girls scrambled out of their bags to prop shoes and wet clothes around the fire for drying. Janice kept singing, and we kept listening. Soon we were all joining in, taking great care to make sure we did not interfere with her amazing voice. When the fire finally died down, it was well past midnight, and everyone was asleep in a matter of minutes.

The next few days were a rainy blur. It was too wet for much hiking. Keeping the fire going was a full-time job, and we were all cold and wet to our core. The trip ended a day early with the promise of many more activities to come. I do remember the actual drive home, because there was so much singing and laughing. Our wild, wet adventure took on a life of its own getting more dangerous and detailed with each telling.

When summer ended, we formed a teen group of girls. There were six in the group with Janice that first year, but our numbers eventually swelled to twenty-two. Twice a month, we would gather to spend the weekend together. Sometimes we just hung out, but more often there were specific activities scheduled that we thought would appeal to teen girls. We went on a dune buggy expedition in the sand dunes along the Oregon coast. We enjoyed shopping at a distant mall, horseback riding, and white water rafting.

On one occasion, we entered the annual Rogue River Great Raft Race in southern Oregon. The race started on the outskirts of Gold Hill and ended safely a few miles downstream. That section of the river is perfect for amateurs. Thankfully, there were no death-defying waterfalls or crazy turbulence pictured in many heart-pounding river rafting movies. It would be an exciting, new experience for our team – without the pitfalls of getting sucked into one of those whirlpools under dangerous places guaranteeing no good outcome.

The girls really wanted to be listed as an all girls' team. There were several categories, mostly divided around age, gender and number of rafters. That created a real problem because we were desperate to have a strong guide in the boat to serve as our rudder. With Janice as the lead spokesperson, they talked the only man on staff into joining our ladies' team. The girls decided to wear blue shorts and pink shirts to live up to our princess reputation. Dressing our male guide into an extra-large pink sleeveless number, fitting him with a long curly blonde wig and providing chest padding that would make any Playboy Bunny proud, we were ready to go. We came in second in our division – the judges agreeing to bend the "all girls" rule for the sake of the team. Janice wept openly and declared, "I've never been this happy."

At every weekend event, we attended church on Sunday morning. That was our rule, and Janice knew it. One Sunday, she decided to drag her feet. She woke up slowly and shuffled her way into the bathroom, locking the door behind her. When I announced that we were leaving in five minutes, Janice shouted through the door, "I'm not going. Not to *that* church."

I explained to her the rule we had made months earlier about attending church, but she would not budge. Finally, I stated with as firm a voice as I could muster, "Janice. I'm taking the rest of the girls to church, and when I return, I will take you home. This will be your last trip with us."

We were all in the van and backing out of the driveway when Janice exploded from the house, her blouse not yet buttoned, her pants unzipped and shoes in hand. A towel was wrapped around her still wet hair.

"Can I change my mind?" With a nod from me, she climbed aboard, and the rest of the girls helped her with buttons, hair and make-up. She clung to me as we walked into the high school room for a very well-prepared program.

It would be more than a year before I discovered why she was so reluctant to attend church that particular morning. One of their associate pastors told her months before when she went with her mother to seek counsel that, "Sexually abused girls make way too much of their abuse."

Janice decided to follow Christ shortly after high school, and I felt certain her life would take a positive turn. But, there were several years of homelessness, tragic disappointments and an eventual marriage to a heroin addict. The last time we talked she called to inform me that the love of her life had died of a drug overdose. I repeatedly begged her to come and stay with me for a few weeks during this most difficult time in her life. She repeatedly promised that she would – "as soon as I get my truck fixed."

Within a few days, an early morning phone call from her mother asked me if I would conduct Janice's funeral services, as she too had died from a heroin overdose. As I openly wept and called everyone I knew that knew her, I could only think of how the world was diminished that day.

Her funeral service was filled with tie-dye shirts, pierced noses and tattoos (long before piercing and tattoos entered the main-stream), leather jackets with obscene words and those dressed to the hilt. We laughed and cried together remembering a child of God with a voice that soared with the angels.

Janice had touched all of us. We came from such an amazing variety of complex and diverse backgrounds, but it didn't seem to matter. Some of her favorite songs were played, and there were many tributes to her incredibly giving spirit. She had changed every one of us in some way.

I cannot remember what I said. I do remember reading God's Word and His plan for His children. There was an open microphone time that lasted more than an hour. We all just wanted to share how much we would miss her, how she had given of herself to all of us and how badly we would long to hear her voice and see her smile one more time.

The pain of any self-inflicted death probably never completely goes away. Questions remained in the hearts of everyone that day. Why couldn't she see herself as all of us saw her – a beautiful child created in the image of God? Why couldn't she see that she had chosen a permanent solution to a temporary problem? What could I have done to give her reason for Hope and a Future? How badly I wanted to return to that crazy, wet, cold backpacking trip, turn back the clock and call for a do-over.

No one wanted to leave after the service concluded. It was as if as long as we stayed together, Janice would stay with us. Several shared some very funny stories. Others wanted all of us to know that Janice was responsible for so much joy in their lives – mine included.

Several hours later, one by one, people started to drift sadly away. One young woman sat quietly in a corner, rocking gently back and forth. As I approached hoping to say something of encouragement, she looked up at me. Her face, already smeared badly where tears and make-up collided, was pale – almost colorless, and there was a real sense of desperation. I sat down next to her and said nothing wanting to wrap my arms around her while respecting her privacy.

She kept rocking back and forth quietly moaning to herself. Finally she looked up at me and spoke, "You said today that

Janice is with God. Forever. How do you know?" And before I had a chance to answer, she continued, "I did lots of drugs with Janice. Mostly crack and marijuana. We were pretty out of it a couple of weeks ago. I don't want to die like that. Not before I know the God thing you spoke about."

Lord, may my heart be broken by what breaks your heart. I know you are weeping right now. Janice made some very bad choices, and she paid dearly for them. I have to believe that even in her death, you had a plan. Please don't let this opportunity in front of me right now slip away. Give me the words – your words.

THE GRASSHOPPER

The first day at camp can be a defining moment – particularly with young boys. It quickly becomes clear those vying for a leadership role, those willing to fit in anywhere and those simply not caring about any of that. Charles was a youngster who simply had too much to see and experience to care much about becoming a part of anyone's pecking order. He had a shock of red hair and wore thick glasses that covered most of his freckled face. The name "four-eyes" didn't seem to bother him. He had been called "four-eyes" for as long as he could remember. Charles wasn't going to let anyone – let alone a bunch of unruly campers his own age – ruin the magic of that week. There were simply too many distractions and too much excitement at every turn.

Everything was a new adventure. He made tiny stick and paper sailboats for his pretend fighting pirates. He discovered that if you were the first to visit the pond in the early morning, you had a good chance of seeing a turtle, neck extended, sunning on a partially submerged log. He found canoes tip over when you try to stand up in them. Most of the time, Charles darted from activity to activity. It really didn't matter if the activity's origin had come from the camp staff or was just something he thought up on his own. He enthusiastically threw himself into everything.

Charles loved grasshoppers and the camp dog.

That week the dog took on the role of camp psychiatrist. He had a keen sense when to sit quietly, place his Golden Retriever head in a child's lap and just listen and when to go full out in a game of catch or tag.

The dog had endless energy – until the evening. At the nightly camp fire, he would lie so still, completely exhausted from his hard day's work, that campers would come over quietly to lay a small hand on his ribs to make sure he was still breathing.

Charles and that dog had a special relationship. There was a sense of commitment, one for the other. Maybe it was because they shared the same name (although we called the dog Charlie) or maybe just because Charlie sensed that Charles needed a little more from him. There was always a stick to fetch or a simple game of tag and chase to play.

One morning Charles tied a bright red bandana around Charlie's neck. The dog would have nothing to do with the makeshift patch Charles tried to put over one of his eyes. After all, don't all pirates wear a bright red bandana and a patch over one eye? Charles eventually gave up and wore the patch himself as they trudged across the field in search of buried treasure or special booty they captured from unsuspecting pirates (campers who had no idea they were part of the game.) Their screams of, "Give it back!" only enhanced the thrill of the chase. When Charles was finally interrupted by the sound of the horn signaling a new activity – lunch and eventually an all-camp game – he returned the booty to the rightful owners, shrugging his shoulders and stated as a matter-of-fact, "It's just a game."

One of the hallmark activities at camp is centered on cooking and eating meals together by tipi teams. The children did all the cooking, table setting and inviting a guest from members of our support staff. That chosen guest is assigned the duty of judging the meal on taste, friendliness and politeness of the team, and actually how well the team all ate together. For many campers, this is a longed-for but completely new experience missing from their home life. It offers the chance to talk about what is going on with each child, laugh together, be a family and feel a sense of accomplishment. It also gives the not-so-athletic camper a chance to shine. Kids good at cooking when mealtime rolls around have a certain status with their teammates unequalled even among the star ball players, swimmers and rock climbers.

Some teams go all out to escort their guest to the tipi site. There is a welcoming song and some pretty amazing table decorations – all created by campers. The centerpiece on the table might include an enormous bouquet of wild flowers or fir cones spelling out the name of their guest or banana slugs collected for such an occasion as this, or even a bucket full of frogs that when the bucket lid is removed make their exit as quickly as possible and in every direction!

On the night Charles' team was cooking hamburgers for dinner, he was given the task of molding one hamburger patty for a guest of his choosing and inviting that guest to join the team – someone from among those of us on the supporting staff. He took his newfound job seriously. While he was walking the distance from his tipi site to the staff tent about two hundred yards away, he worked diligently to form the perfect burger – right size, right shape, and Charles declared, "Perfect... everything!"

As he worked on his molding project, he surveyed the group of us and walked straight up to me. "My team, the Brave Warriors, would like to invite you to join us for dinner." Before I had a chance to respond, Charles spied Charlie resting in the shade of a large pine tree. Charlie had a rough afternoon.

Several boys decided to test his swimming skills counting that the *retriever* in him would kick in and never miss an opportunity to go swimming *and* fetch, all in one game. They kept the game going for well over an hour. Charlie was exhausted. He lay almost motionless, but as Charles approached, he wagged his tail and raised his head as if to say, "For you, Charles, I'll play more catch if that is what you want to do."

Charles plopped down next to the exhausted dog and intermittently divided his attention between his hamburger masterpiece and the animal he had grown to love. While Charlie licked the grease from his hands, Charles kept working on the hamburger. His glasses slid off his nose, and any leftover grease found its way onto the lens until it was fairly certain he had extremely limited vision. When someone offered to clean his glasses, he stated that he could see just fine and that he had an assignment he intended to fulfill.

It was clear this dog-licked, dirt-filled hamburger was my intended dinner. It was also clearly too late to back out, and my prayer life took on new meaning. *Lord, you know how much I like crispy burned bacon. Let it be so with that hamburger tonight!*

The next morning, Charles decided it was time to pursue his dream of catching and training a grasshopper. The meadow was loaded with them. Grasshoppers of every size. Catching the right one for the assignment was no easy task for a boy with greased-up glasses. Most boys would have given up.

I watched Charles in hot pursuit for nearly an hour until a camper with an imbedded splinter diverted my attention.

About twenty minutes later, Charles came running at full speed toward the staff tent. One hand was clenched into a tight fist, the other desperately trying to straighten his glasses over at least one eye. "Marilyn, come quick."

I ran over to where he was standing, a broad grin on his face. He slowly opened his clenched fist to let me see up close what he had captured. Perhaps the largest grasshopper I have ever seen lay on its side, gasping for the last breath that had almost been squeezed out of it. As he gently stroked his new pet with one finger, he proclaimed, "Look! I have him trained."

God has a way of weaving stories into our lives for us to see and learn from or totally ignore. It is always our call. Watching a kid like Charles at camp that week, those lessons were blatantly obvious. He served as a reminder to find joy in even the most unexpected places, to stretch our imagination as far as we can and not to take ourselves too seriously.

The Nursing Home Pig

The drive up Highway 5 from California to Oregon is long, and the six teen girls in the van with me were more than anxious to get going. This new adventure, one of many, might just be what was needed to turn an upside down life, right side up. They were delighted to leave the San Francisco Bay area and the personal abuse and neglect that had dogged their daily routine. Some were escaping yet another foster home. Others were dodging another one of mom's unwelcome boyfriends.

All six girls had experienced sexual abuse. Though it never serves as a bonding agent, they have that one thing in common. They long for their lives to be different. Reality dictates their lives may never be different. Memories always have some stickiness to them. They are hard to shake off.

The first half of the trip through the Sacramento Valley offered little excitement. "Too flat and too hot," as one girl put it. My co-pilot was fidgety. She wanted to share her discomfort as well as her life story with everyone who would listen.

"I didn't get any sleep last night. My boyfriend wanted – well, you probably know what he wanted." I was pretty sure where she was going with this but decided to keep my comments to myself and just listen. Sarah had bounced through several foster homes, a lock-up facility and a group home. Now she was back with her mother with a definite lack of supervision. Sarah wanted me to know that mom had her own life, which did not include an out-of-control teenager.

While five girls slept restlessly in the back seats, Sarah told me details of the abusive life that had become her normal, mostly at the hands of her mother, now her primary caregiver. The apartment was always dark, always smoke-filled and always noisy. It had but one bedroom, so Sarah slept on the living room couch. I had to wonder how well social services had done with their parental background checks.

The last three hours of our trip, we crossed Lake Shasta and then drove through the majestic Cascade Mountains. Even inner-city girls find jaw-dropping moments of scenery. Mt. Shasta, clearly visible towering above us off Highway 5, was still covered in snow. We vowed to at least make a quick stop on our way back home. (Although when we actually passed by on our return trip, they were less enthusiastic and opted to keep driving.)

Seven hours after our departure, we pulled into the driveway of an incredible, magical farm – our destination. We would call the farm our home for the next six days. The farm owner spoke briefly about expectations, but mostly he wanted all of us to know we were most welcome. It would clearly offer a chance for a bit of normalcy and rest.

Knowing how important it is for vulnerable teens to experience giving to others, we decided to visit a local nursing home – with two baby pigs. The pigs came from the farm, and the girls knew they would be well received.

Getting them ready for the trip and their debut from the farm to the nursing home was a full-blown ordeal. The girls assumed that pigs would be more than appreciative to receive the complete bubble bath and manicure treatment. There were wild chases around the backyard, squealing pigs, very wet teen girls and lots of laughter. It is always good to hear laughter with hurting children, particularly teen girls, because often that is the first thing to disappear in dysfunctional families. By the time we were loaded up and headed to the nursing home, the pigs were reasonably clean and definitely presentable.

There were a few heated discussions on the drive into town to decide which two girls would carry the pigs. They settled on the two oldest. It seemed to be a fair decision, and I was extremely happy I was not asked to be the referee. No one could have prepared us for what lay ahead as we entered the main area where residents of the nursing home were being wheeled in for our grand entrance.

The average age must have been in the low to mid eighties. Several smiled slightly when they saw the pigs; others never looked up. One woman shared a lengthy childhood memory of her grandfather's farm and a summer visit. "I had to feed pigs just like this one." She touched it tenderly with gnarled fingers as she drifted off to her grandfather's farm many years ago.

One of our TYM girls lingered near hoping to hear a little more. Within moments, she fell asleep with the pig squirming in her arms until it was extracted and passed on to the next resident.

As we were winding through the waiting line toward the last resident, the girls were getting a little fidgety and seemed ready to pack up the pigs and head back to the farm. At that moment, one more resident was wheeled into the room. She was the youngest resident – by at least thirty years. Her dark hair and crooked smile went almost unnoticed. One might rightfully have guessed that someone had removed her spine and most of the bones surrounding it. She was simply piled into the wheelchair. One useless arm lay at an uncomfortable angle. Fingers were curved in an awkward position, looking as if they were attached with a rather poor grade adhesive and now were slowly slipping off her hand.

Her two feet dragged on the floor threatening to get sucked under the wheelchair at any moment, pulling the rest of her body under along with them. At one point the attendant gently put them back in place on their pedestals. She was dressed for company, the reason for her late entrance. She must have heard a rumor of our appearance with farm animals, and it had taken every minute since our arrival for a caring attendant to change her into something she felt would be appropriate for an occasion such as this.

One of the employees at the home pulled me aside. "Joanne was in a horrible automobile accident several years ago and was not expected to live. She was in a coma for a very long time. In spite of the round-the-clock medication we give her, she is in pain 100% of the time. If you could just stay a little bit longer, I know it would mean the world to her to see and hold one of the pigs."

Our teens sensed this was important and did not hesitate. They quickly walked over to where Joanne was sitting, crumpled in her wheelchair. They gently placed one of the pigs in her lap. The pig squirmed slightly, and Joanne began to smile. Her lips curled on one side revealing the absence of most of her teeth undoubtedly knocked out in the car accident. She tried to maneuver one hand in a way to actually stroke the little piglet but could not make it work. Two girls wanted to help her out, but it seemed awkward. They didn't know where to begin. This was brand new territory, and they surely did not want to attempt anything that might end up an embarrassment. I wondered if I should intervene – if all this was just a little too much for Joanne, but our persistent teens were not about ready to leave. They refused to make eye contact with me, should I decide to call it a day. We all were waiting for the Joanne story and the inevitable lesson to come. She did not disappoint us.

Before long our entire group – leaders and teens – were sitting at the foot of the wheelchair, hanging on to two baby pigs and waiting for Joanne to say something – anything. As she spoke, her mouth drifted uncontrollably to the left, and she began to drool slightly. Her words tumbled out barely understandable, and she spoke so softly that we had to lean close to her, wanting to make sure not to miss a word. We clearly had never met anyone like her. Instead of repulsion at the look of her, we were drawn magically toward the light in her eyes.

"Five year ago, I was a very bitter, angry young woman. I had a great job, making lots of money, but I was selfish and miserable. My husband had just left me, and I found myself alone. Then three years ago, I was in a terrible automobile accident. No one expected me to live."

The girls were transfixed by what she was telling them. Beauty, fame, fortune. It was the very thing they longed for in their own lives, and now it was all gone in one short horrible moment. It could happen to anyone!

Now, Joanne began to cry softly, as if remembering the details of her accident brought on a deep sadness. "I was in a coma for a very long time. When I woke up, I could not move anything. And I was angry. So angry. I hated everyone. Refused to talk to anyone. I knew God was punishing me for all the mistakes I had made."

Joanne stopped talking. It took every ounce of her limited energy to stumble through her words. She just needed a short break to recuperate. We sat motionless while Joanne dozed off for several seconds – not that deep catnap sleep but rather dozing to regroup her thoughts.

Suddenly, she jerked her head to a nearly straight position and continued, "The first year I was here, I barely spoke to anyone. Not even my nurses who bathed and fed me and did all those things to keep me alive. Then one day, one of the nurses told me about Jesus. I didn't want to hear, but deep down I knew she was right. Jesus is the best thing that has ever happened to me. It took my accident to figure that out. Do all of you know Jesus?"

There was a moment of painful silence. How do you tell a woman who has just poured out her life story that you are a punk teenage girl doing drugs whenever you can? How do you tell her that you don't want to know Jesus because you are afraid of the lifestyle you are sure God will make you give up?

Two girls began to cry and leaned closer to Joanne. It was an amazing picture – two heads and two small pigs all vying for attention.

After several quiet moments, Joanne spoke. "I know you are struggling. You are just like I was. But you need Jesus. You need Jesus. He rescued me, and I know he wants to be part of your life too."

Every girl clearly saw the obvious. Beauty had been taken away. Fame and fortune soon followed. But in the process, God found a home, and His light was shining brightly.

On the drive home, one of the teens confessed, "You know, I am a lot like our pigs. I can clean up on the outside, but on my inside, I'm still the same old me." Another added, "Yeah, but I read somewhere that pigs get dirty for a reason. It keeps their skin from getting a sunburn, and it also keeps them cool."

The discussion continued, "Do you think we sometimes get dirty for a reason?" It was evident what they were saying had less to do with their outward appearance. They had seen firsthand how the outward appearance could be crushed almost beyond recognition, but the inside was an entirely different story. Joanne and the light surrounding her were more compelling than anything they had yet to experience. It had been a *"moth drawn to the light of a candle"*

One of the girls wistfully spoke – almost thinking out loud. "If Jesus could rescue Joanne, you think maybe He could rescue me?"

JAMAL

Four vans arrived just about the same time in the camp parking lot. That is not always a good thing. When thirty-six, eight to twelve year old boys hit the ground at the same time, a pecking order is immediately established before the camp has even had a chance to get underway. It was very clear to all of us that Jamal was at the top of the chain and would be our biggest challenge.

Jamal waited in the van until all the gear was unloaded. As he stepped with precision onto the ground, all the other boys parted to give him whatever space he needed. He was a very big twelve-year-old – considerably overweight – and he stood a clear head above the other campers. Jamal gave the shoulder shrug that announced to our camp staff that he in fact was in charge – of everything. Two other boys picked up his belongings and loaded them into the truck for transport into the tipi village. Jamal didn't acknowledge the act of kindness. It was expected.

When the boys were instructed to pick teams (six campers and two team leaders that would live together for the week), they carefully avoided Jamal. He folded his arms and stared at the ground as if he expected to be courted by every team. When it was suddenly apparent that he might not be chosen at all, his eyes darted frantically to position himself on the team of his choice. He casually walked over to one group, and you could see the relief in six pair of eyes. Their team was full. Rather than face a possible second rejection, Jamal did a quick head count, shrugged his shoulders and moved to the team that was still one short. They accepted him without comment.

Walking from the parking lot to the tipi village gave us a glimpse of our week with Jamal. He did what he wanted, at the pace that he wanted with no regard for his two bewildered team leaders. They were not prepared for the likes of Jamal, and quite frankly, in spite of years of experience and training, no one else on staff was either. We could only guess what his life must have been like to bring him to this point.

Jamal's teammates barely tolerated him. They shot glances at each other to see which one would be forced into the role of Jamal's slave for the day. They all knew the unspoken rules. If you didn't want to get beaten up in the dead of night, you let Jamal do all the leading and all the deciding. Camp activities took a backseat to maintaining a semblance of order on the team. Whenever possible, one by one, the boys would slip away to join another team – it really didn't matter what they were doing as long as "the bully" was not a part of it! All the other teams, relieved that Jamal was not a part of their team, welcomed his teammates mostly with deep empathy for the lot they were dealt.

On the morning of the third day, the bathroom clean up crew reported that someone had written the "f" word on a wall in one of the outhouses, and it looked as if it had been written with human feces. We all had our suspicions as to the responsible party, but without a DNA test, there really was no concrete proof. We cleaned up the writing, repainted the outhouse and said nothing.

Jamal was fidgety most of that morning. It was as if he were waiting for someone to accuse him of the bathroom mess. He avoided all camp activities and for once kept to himself. His teammates were grateful to be left alone. In the early afternoon, one of his team leaders reported that someone had written the "f" word on the inside of their tipi wall, and it was also suspected to be human feces.

We cleaned it up during the afternoon swimming session. I walked into the tipi area as Jamal's team was putting the finishing touches on their dinner, and he gave me the look that screamed, "Well, what are you going to do about it?" He proceeded to announce that the camp was a mess and that someone needed to take charge. I gently laid my hand on Jamal's shoulder and assured him that I could handle almost anything and that he need not worry because we had everything under control.

Now visibly angry, Jamal reached up and rudely ripped my hand off his shoulder. My little finger caught his imitation gold necklace, and it went flying, landing in the dirt behind him. He leapt to his feet, shouting obscenities at me while threatening to take me to court, along with the camp, the team leaders and my family in perpetuity. Jamal stomped into the tipi and threw his belongs into the paper sack that served as his suitcase. As he stormed off, he swore and emphatically stated, "I'm leaving this f_ing place. This camp sucks!" And he started walking down the road.

When Today's Youth Matter (TYM) was given the use of our camp property from Big Creek Lumber Company, one thing was very clear. No child in his or her right mind would actually succeed in a foot escape from camp. It was a five-mile trek to the front gate along an abandoned logging road – and rumors continued to circulate that if the wild boars and rattlesnakes didn't get you, surely you would die in the jaws of a mountain lion or perhaps even Big Foot.

Jamal had walked about 200 yards when it occurred to him the length of the walk in front of him. You could see him mentally calculating the distance he could cover before darkness set in and all those wild animals would begin to prowl. As his pace slowed, one of the older men on staff walked up to him to try and defuse his anger. After about an hour, he was able to accept my apology for breaking his necklace and even acknowledged it was probably an accident.

That was a turning point. Jamal participated with his team for the first time in their campfire skit that night. And according to the team leaders reporting the following morning to our leadership team, he crawled into his sleeping bag without a word. After the morning staff meeting, team leaders returned to wake up their campers and cook breakfast. Jamal actually helped with the clean up.

It was clearly going to be a hot day – one of those scorchers that weathermen love to talk about on the radio. By mid-morning we agreed that a trip into the cool canyon and cooler water below was in order. It was a short walk down a steep trail, but it was an adventure, and surely Big Foot would respect our numbers.

We gathered on the ball field and explained that for most of the fifteen-minute trek, we would have to walk single file. The trail was well marked, but maneuvering thirty-six campers and eighteen adults down the steep terrain called for teamwork, patience, a certain level of cooperation and a bit of luck. I was in the front trying to slow down the boys who were only interested in reaching the creek first and encourage the slower boys, distracted by lizards, small bugs and any other moveable creature to keep up with the rest of us.

The very last part of the hike broke out into a lovely meadow. At its far edge was the steep embankment to the road directly next to the creek. About one-third of our group traversed the meadow without incident. I was hoping that we could form a human chain to allow the whole group to slide down the final steep pitch. Suddenly several loud screams pierced the air from the meadow. It didn't take long to realize that one of the boys had stepped into a hornet's nest, and they were under attack.

Immediately, panic set in. Boys were plunging toward the embankment out of control with hornets in hot pursuit. All the leaders were yelling for the campers to "Slow down" before they hit the embankment at full speed. I began to mentally calculate the pile up below if we could not get everyone deliberately to plan those last fifty yards.

Amidst the screams, I looked up, and there was Jamal. His feet were planted about three feet apart, and he was catching the boys one by one as they tumbled toward him. He did not say a word, but his actions spoke volumes. In a matter of seconds disaster was averted, and we were at the stream cooling off a few hornet stings (or do they bite?) and sharing harrowing stories of near death at the hands of such tiny creatures.

Jamal passed me with a nod, and I returned the nod with a smile to acknowledge what he had done. At that moment, I knew we would probably never become best friends, but at least we were no longer enemies.

The boys played in the cool creek for about an hour before someone suggested it was time for our picnic lunch. There was a great sandy beach on the other side of the creek where peanut butter sandwiches, chips, fruit and cookies distracted everyone long enough to abandon the search for salamanders and snakes to cross the small stream. One of the leaders had placed large rocks in the water. Although the water's depth could not have been more than six inches, and everyone had been wading in it for the full hour with their "creek stomping sneakers," the boys were happy to use the rocks. All except for Daniel.

Daniel was a "special needs" camper and was liked by almost everyone. He suffered partial paralysis from infancy at the hands of one of mom's angry boyfriends who, in a moment of rage, slammed him against a wall. Daniel walked with a severe limp, and as he tentatively reached the water's edge, he must have realized he had little chance of crossing the stream without falling repeatedly. He hesitated just long enough for Jamal to catch up to him, and without any words or hesitation, Jamal swept him up in his arms and stomped across the stream, gently depositing him in the sand on the other side. Daniel smiled his thanks, and Jamal acknowledged it with a nod.

At our final awards ceremony, Jamal's team leaders nominated him for the "Camp Director's Award" given to the most improved and best all round camper. He was the unanimous choice of all the leadership. We felt we had witnessed a miracle. Jamal smiled for a split second, but caught himself. Instead he nodded his approval at receiving the honor as though he could hardly imagine that someone could actually believe in him enough for the nomination. All the campers clapped loudly.

As Jamal neared his van for the trip home, I thought for a moment he might give me a hug. Instead he tapped my shoulder and whispered, "Camp was fun." There were so many things I wanted to tell him but never had the chance or maybe even the courage. "You are one remarkable young man." "Leave your toughness here at camp." "Come to snow camp and join one of our small groups." "I will NEVER forget you, Jamal." "You have taught me so much about myself. I know God has His grip on your life." "You are the same child of God as the rest of us. You deserve someone to believe in you."

He climbed into the van, eyes watering, not wanting me to see the crushing disappointment of going home to tougher circumstances than he thought I could handle. I gave him a "thumbs up," an encouraging smile and waved until the van was out of sight.

His mother disappeared a week after the camp ended. It is hard to tell what drove her from where they were living. I can only guess it might have been her own abusive background with too many boyfriends or too many bill collectors. I never saw Jamal again, and often wonder if he took the lessons from camp into adulthood. Although it would never be *my* first choice, I am trying to learn to be content with the knowledge he is indeed in God's tender grip.

Karate and Jesus

I love to watch tough young boys the first day of camp. They have that street savvy that screams, "I am not scared of anything! Not you. Not this camp. Not anything!" That is until the sun goes down, and I have the flashlight! The toughest kid turns into a clinging vine – my new best friend.

Diana was definitely *not* one of those kids. From the moment she arrived at camp, I knew there was a genuine fear that tenaciously gripped her to her core. Without extensive intake, it was almost impossible to nail down the origin of her fear. I didn't even try. My job that week was to surround her with the very type of love God extends to us – no questions asked. Through her fear, she was certain that her very survival was in fact placed in my hands, and she clung to me as if her life depended upon it.

I liked her immediately. I wished only for her to experience the joy of catching a first fish, of swimming the width of the pool, of maneuvering the high ropes' course and of trapping a lizard or salamander. With every step her large brown eyes darted frantically at the ground in front of her, at the trees and birds above her and at every noise she heard. I found myself listening with her for sounds I took for granted – crickets, bullfrogs, birds and insects. When we take the time, God's creation becomes alive in a way we never dream possible. Sounds and sights are everywhere. It is important to just slow down and take the time to look and listen!

At our first campfire, I sensed Diana was in trouble. Although she sat with her two team leaders, she knew that I knew the camp well and trusted as long as I was close by, nothing would happen to her. I moved over next to her, and she crawled onto my lap for a good part of our time of songs, skits and a brief Bible lesson. When the campfire ended, I gave her my very bright flashlight and reminded her that her three leaders would definitely take care of her and look out for her best interest. They had my permission to come and get me at a moment's notice during the night. Reluctantly, Diana trudged off with her team back to their tipi, glancing in my direction until she was out of sight.

After a trip to the bathroom, "Goodnights" all around and prayers for a good night's sleep, the team leaders announced it was time to turn off all flashlights. Getting little giggling, nervous girls to quiet down on the first night of camp is no easy task. Between the laughter and "I think I have to go to the bathroom again" and "Can I have a drink of water?" it takes time and patience to say the final "Good night" and believe the day has at last come to an end.

One team leader recounted this story at our staff meeting the following morning.

"I think it took us nearly an hour to get the girls settled into their sleeping bags. We all prayed repeatedly with each girl for a good night's rest and safety in all our activities the next morning. The flashlights were finally turned off, and everyone was beginning to fall asleep when Diana turned on her light and whispered, "What's that?" I tried to assure her it was probably just a cricket or something really harmless, and it was dark again – for the next minute or so. Her light flashed around the tipi, and she seemed to see something crawling above her head. She now began to whimper and cry. I tried again to comfort her, so before the whimper turned into a full-blown "I'm going to die" wail, I moved my sleeping bag next to hers. She seemed to be settling down once again when we heard the hoot of an owl. Again her light went on making sure there would be no owl intrusions into the tipi. She made me check to see that the tipi door flap was secure.

"Again, it was dark, and I was just starting to fall asleep when Diana grabbed my arm, turned on her flashlight and stated that she knew there was a raccoon in the tipi. After a complete search of the circular walls, we found nothing. I was slightly exasperated, and I told her emphatically, "Diana, we are all black belts in karate, and anyway.... we know Jesus."

A few seconds later, Diana leaned over and whispered, "But, does Jesus know karate?"

Eric

During Today's Youth Matter's (TYM) first six years, without a camp of our own, we were forced to rent a variety of facilities. We used four different sites during those years.

Some had certain endearing qualities – a large lake for swimming and boating, an extra large campfire circle, an amazing waterslide, several natural creeks – but all were lacking the same thing. They did not feel like home.

At one site in the rolling hills near Marysville, California, the camp was filled to capacity. The team leaders were a bit overwhelmed with the number of tough boys – four of them from one family. Eric was their self-appointed leader. He was fourteen and had somehow slipped through our age regulation of just eight to twelve year old campers.

There is a huge difference between a small eight year old and a tall fourteen year old. Eric did his best to exploit his age and size. Three cousins – or so he told us – were also at camp, and they had a secret sign language that allowed them all to be on the same page before they actually began their reign of terror.

Toward the beginning of the week, Eric let us know that as long as he could ride the best bicycle in camp and take it away from any other camper at any time, he would do his best to limit his most damaging behavior. That self-restraint did not include intimidation, small shoves and pushes or any of the colorful words he chose to let fly.

There were some wonderful moments with Eric and the entire camp. One evening, we encouraged the boys to sleep on the expansive lawn that surrounded the campfire circle. There was an expected meteor shower that night, and we knew that a spectacular light show was in store. Most TYM campers rarely ever see stars. Trapped in the inner city with too many night-lights, stargazing is limited to recognizing there might be something up there, but it probably will turn out to be just an airplane.

The boys jumped at the opportunity to change their night venue and discover yet another "first" for themselves. Sleeping bags were pulled out of the cabins, and laid in a patchwork design on the lawn. No one seemed to care about the uneven terrain. They were ready to experience the show they hoped would rival anything ever seen on the fourth of July.

One of the leaders backed his pick-up truck onto the lawn and suggested that some of us could sleep in the bed of the truck that was covered with thick padding. Everyone over forty raced for a spot.

All of a sudden Eric showed up and, after waiting in the wings for his grand entrance, he made a beeline for his chosen spot in a slight depression where the grass appeared softest. It made no difference that several young campers already had their sleeping bags laid out and occupied his predetermined destination. Before anyone on staff had the opportunity to intervene, the boys scrambled to get out of his way. They knew the consequences of making even the slightest objection.

As they were settling into their sleeping bags waiting for the light show to begin, one of the nervous younger boys asked a simple question. "Are there any rattlesnakes around here?" The older boys responded as expected, "You afraid, you little baby?" "You need your mommy to protect you?" "Boy, you don't know anything."

Several of our staff looked at each other and smiled. This was *way* too easy.

Quietly, we began a conversation about rattlesnakes; if we had seen any in the last twenty-four hours at camp; how many were in the area; what kind of rattlesnakes they were and how often they were likely to strike. Suddenly, the lawn area became dead silent. Surely even a slithering snake through the grass could be detected. Every camper was 100% focused on our conversation.

Finally, one nervous voice poised the question every camper wanted to ask.

"Are there rattlesnakes around here?"

The deepest adult voice spoke with authority. "This kind of country is loaded with them. It's exactly the type of place they like to live. It's the perfect environment for them."

"Snakes don't come out at night...do they?"

"Well, they do feed at night. And they are attracted to light."

Several voices spoke in a loud whisper, "Turn off your flashlight. Turn off your flashlight!"

"And heat! It's a pretty warm night, but I'm guessing they'll be looking for the warmest spot around here."

In unison, forty-two boys scrambled out of their warm sleeping bags and piled into the bed of the pick-up and onto the hood – anywhere away from sleeping bags and impending death. We were laughing so hard, it didn't seem to matter that all those bodies were crushing us. (The next morning we did take the time to correct the record about the eating and sleeping habits of California rattlesnakes. For some strange reason, the boys could not quite understand our adult humor.)

Eric participated in a basic water safety class and actually appeared to learn something he could hang onto. At the end of the class, we set up a fake water emergency close to shore, and the boys knew exactly what to do. With Eric barking out commands, they quickly formed a human chain and waded out for their rescue. They were delighted at their stellar performance under pressure, and although there were complaints about being tricked with our "pretend drowning", we were quickly forgiven amidst words of congratulations.

On the fourth day of camp, Eric exploded. He began throwing rocks and recruited his cousins and a few others to follow suit. Safety is always the number one concern at camp, and Eric was physically separated from the other campers to an isolated area for a serious conversation. I thought he understood the consequences of his actions. Rock throwing would not be tolerated, and he would be sent home immediately if it continued.

There were a couple of peaceful hours, but some careless word thrown in Eric's direction prompted more rocks and fists. Eric was told to pack up his belongings. In spite of the fact there was less than twenty-four hours left at camp, we were taking him home.

At first, he smiled. His face communicated that he had gotten the attention he wanted. He went to grab his cousins, and when he realized they had no intention of leaving with him – camp was way too fun – Eric fell apart. His world appeared to be crumbling.

Eric began to cry uncontrollably, begging to stay and promising to be on his best behavior. He sat down next to me, and I tried to explain that every action, good and bad, has a consequence. All of us experience consequences for our actions. If I eat too much I gain weight. If I exercise consistently, I get stronger. While he was going home immediately, he didn't have to carry his negative behavior with him everywhere, and we at TYM would do everything in our power to help him along the way.

With my two hands, I pointed in opposite directions. "Eric, you are at a crossroads. Take the road you are on (and I pointed to the left) and you are undoubtedly headed toward a very tough life – maybe even prison or death. It doesn't have to be like that. Take the other road – (and I pointed to the right) – and you can be anything you want to be. God has a life-changing plan for you. I hope we will stay in contact. TYM will help you every step of the way, and I will be praying for you."

He looked up at me and, through understanding eyes, responded, "I choose this one," and he touched my right hand. He gave me a half-hug and slowly climbed into the car for the three-hour ride home.

Eric remained part of the program through his sophomore year of high school. I never saw him fight at any of our activities, although I am not naïve enough to think that his fighting days were over. It just takes time. Lots and lots of time. And patience. Lots and lots of patience. Galatians 5:22 – 23 comes to mind. (*"But the fruit of the spirit is love, joy, peace, patience, kindness, goodness, faithfulness, gentleness and self-control. Against such things there is no law." (NIV)*

Not The Hill

Life lessons rarely occur in a classroom setting. Lectures just can't seem to bring it home. But when a child somehow latches onto something he or she will carry into adulthood – often in the most unexpected place and at the most unexpected time – you can almost see the light bulb turn on. After many years in ministry work, it is what I long for. Months and sometimes years of unsuccessfully trying to steer a child in a new direction melt away, and that is sheer magical bliss.

That magic was working overtime at a snow trip weekend with twenty-six excited, energy-filled little boys. Most of our TYM kids have never seen snow except on television or in the movies. They are surprised that it is so cold; amazed it can sometimes be fluffy and soft in one spot and just a few feet away icy and unforgiving. As expected, keeping waterproof gloves and warm hats on boys in the midst of a snowball fight is not always easy. They rarely remember that 80% of our body heat is dedicated to keeping the brain functional, and fingers and toes are not high on the body's survival chart.

We had traveled to the Sierra Mountains and settled on a snow park with several decent inner tube runs. Of course, we were not alone. In fact, the park was packed. I just had to pray that our diligent volunteers and staff would keep eyes open to make sure we didn't lose anyone. I was prepared for cold feet, unzipped and eventually discarded jackets, wet gloves and mittens and the usual variety of questions: "Are they selling hot chocolate?" "Can we get some now?" I was not prepared for the angry father that was rapidly headed straight toward me.

He stopped just inches from my face. "Are you in charge of these obnoxious kids?" It was a loaded question, and probably anything I said would not make this extremely uncomfortable situation any better. I nodded my head.

Now most of our TYM boys had gathered around, much the way they do just before a schoolyard fight. This was pretty much a no-win situation, and I shot up a quick prayer. *"Lord, how come you always had the perfect answer when the Pharisees thought they had painted you into a corner with absolutely no way out? Can you loan me one of those answers, because I am about to be eaten alive if I don't think of something brilliant in the next few seconds? Help!!!"*

The father continued, "Two of your boys – those two – said some really offensive things to my little girls. I can't even repeat what they said. Don't they know better? Haven't you taught them words like that are never to be repeated anywhere, least of all in public? They shouldn't be allowed here in the first place." I looked down at his two adorable girls – maybe four and five years old – and could only imagine the words the boys had uttered.

I signaled for the father to follow me away from the circle of TYM boys. The boys started to follow, but I gave them "the look" (the one that says, "Don't even think about it, if you are planning to get a ride home from here"), and they let us slip off just out of earshot but visible just in case I called for help. They were more than prepared to come to my rescue should the need arise. I tried to explain to the man some backgrounds of most of the boys. Somehow, with a promise that we would do our best to keep our children away from everyone else on the hill and profuse apologies for any discomfort his girls had to endure, he shrugged his shoulders and walked away, muttering something about not coming to the mountains with his family for this kind of abuse.

Relieved, I retreated to our kids, in no mood for the high-fives they wanted to give me. I signaled for the two accused of the crime – again, staring down the rest of our group so they would make no attempt to follow.

At first the two – Kareem and Robert – began to protest. "We didn't do anything. That guy's a racist. We just made a few comments that wouldn't hurt a fly. Hey, we can take him if you want. He had no business messing with you like that."

Again, a quick prayer. *"Lord, give me the right words. They have to understand."*

"Guys, I didn't see what happened, and I didn't hear what you said. Evidently, the girls told their dad or he overheard something, and you could tell he wasn't very happy. This has nothing to do with race. It has everything to do with truth and honor and character." They looked quizzically at me, evidently with no clue what I was talking about.

Somehow, I dragged from memory something I had heard from one of the many seminars I had attended at a Christian conference. I continued, "Kareem, Robert, someone once told me to ask the question before doing anything in tough situations. Ask yourself, 'Is this the hill where I'm prepared to die?'"

Robert rolled his eyes, and Kareem started kicking the snow. They had no idea where I was heading. I continued, "Before you do something that may cause deep problems and horrible consequences, ask yourself, 'Is this the hill where I am prepared to die?' My husband has a really ugly shirt, and quite frankly I wish he would throw it away, but I am not prepared to die for his decision to wear it. If the house is on fire and if you guys are trapped inside, I certainly am prepared to go enter that house. If you are trying to swim across the pond at camp, and you start to go under, I'm prepared to die trying to save you. Is this the thing – what you said to those two little girls – where you are prepared to die?"

They looked at each other and then at me and in unison shook their heads sheepishly. There were many other things I wanted to say about controlling their words or never fighting in school, but I decided to leave well enough alone. That could wait for another day.

A few minutes before we left, the father of the girls signaled me to come over to him. Not knowing what was in store,

I moved rather slowly in his direction. His smile was as much from happiness as it was from utter disbelief.

"I'm not sure what you said to those two, but I just wanted you to know, they not only came over and apologized to me, but they actually said they were sorry to my daughters. In fact, one of them loaned his sled to them and even carried it to the top of the hill!"

I didn't know quite how to respond. It was all God and His prompting in their hearts. I muttered something that made little sense and retreated to give Kareem and Robert a high five. They got the lesson, in spite of me.

On the drive home, we stopped for lunch. Kareem wanted to sit next to me and tell me details of his near-death experience going over a wild jump they had built on one of the inner tube runs. It had been a day to remember for him, maybe a life-changer. Not only did he experience the unknown, he had learned an important lesson about kindness and about choosing your battles. Not everything calls for fight mode.

After we had eaten, and before we left for the rest of the drive home, I stated rather emphatically, "Kareem, I have to go to the bathroom. Please guard my purse with your life."

Without a moment's hesitation, he shot back, "Marilyn, this is not the hill where I am prepared to die!"

IN A WHISPER

When TYM was first given an open invitation to bring children to a real southern Oregon farm anytime, we jumped all over it. A number of stories included in this book take place at that Farm.

There were too-many-to-count positives and only one negative. The drive was long taking almost seven hours. We eventually turned that very long trek from the San Francisco Bay area to southern Oregon negative into an adventure in its own right. On hot travel days, we stopped for a brief swim in Lake Shasta – about four hours into the drive. There are at least twelve clean gas station bathrooms, and two Chucky Cheese restaurants I have personally visited along Highway 5 with a vanload of children.

The farm offers lasting memories. Collecting eggs is a favorite for our city dwellers. One youngster raced into the farmhouse, her shirt filled with still warm eggs of every size and color and pulled me aside. "That's got to hurt," she whispered emphatically after watching a hen deposit an egg. When we used them to make an omelet, another girl informed us, "I don't eat those eggs. Only the ones we get from Safeway."

It took a whole lot of convincing these were the same eggs that eventually made their way to the grocery store – just a lot fresher. She *finally* agreed to at least give them a try. She smiled broadly and exclaimed, "I've never had anything like this before. Can I have seconds?"

Horseback riding provides magical moments for every pre-teen who has watched *Black Beauty* or other movies where cowboys and pioneers tame the Wild West. It is a chance to dream of galloping across the green meadow, hair flying in the wind, realizing you and the horse are truly one, and you have not a care in the world.

One ten-year-old, donning a pair of worn, caked-with-mud farm boots and an extremely old hat she found in an abandoned closet, placed one foot firmly on a chair, and in her best John Wayne drawl, looked in the mirror and said, "Well, how you doing there, little lady?"

The lessons from the farm are as varied as the children. Respect the earth. Hard work is actually good for you. Crops won't grow if you never move the irrigation pipes. It is really easy to fall asleep when you have been working all day. Breakfast truly is the most important meal of the day. Fresh vegetables (and farm eggs) taste nothing like the ones you get in the store near your inner-city apartment or house.

The last night on one of our stays, the farm owner and TYM board member, Jack Smith, told a group of girls the story of Elijah. He explained when Elijah told God he was tired and just wanted to die, God brought him to a place to rest. As the story began to unfold, the girls listened intently anxious to find out how it would end for Elijah. When they heard the part that included fire, wind and thunder – and no God, you could see the girls wondering if God would ever come to rescue him in his time of dire need. And perhaps there was a deeper question. "Will God rescue me in my time of need?"

"Then God came to Elijah in a whisper." (1 Kings 19:12 NIV) And the lesson was clear. We *must* be quiet and listen if we want to have a chance to hear God's voice.

After a tearful goodbye, we began our long trek home back to the San Francisco Bay area. Somewhere, as we were traveling over the Siskiyou Mountains, one of the girls sitting in the front seat leaned over and told me, "God came to me in a whisper last night." When I inquired what she heard, she answered, "He said, 'Say kind words.'"

Maybe God was speaking through her to all of us. I can only hope we are listening.

Asleep On The Trail

First impressions are not always correct. My tendency is to like everyone I meet – or at least to give them the benefit of the doubt until they prove me wrong. Mindy was no exception. She was dreadfully pale. Although she was only eight, she might have passed for much younger, except that her long blond, almost white hair must have taken every minute of those eight years to grow. It hung almost to her knees.

The rumors about a bitter life of abuse swirled all around her. She had been in more foster homes than anyone – including her multiple caseworkers – could count. The story was always the same when a new family was interviewed after her departure. "She was just too difficult for us to handle."

By the time she came to her first TYM summer camp, Mindy's behavior was so out of control, her doctors prescribed seven different kinds of medication for her little body, several with multiple doses. She reminded me of what a zombie from one of those dreadful childhood movies looked like: vacant eyes, inability to communicate a clear sentence, and going through each day in a haze.

Her medication routine began before breakfast—one blue pill and two pink pills. At mid-morning, another blue pill, one white pill and one green. The green pill seemed the most difficult to get down, perhaps because of its size or perhaps because Mindy knew its effect on her. There were more pills at lunch, during the mid-afternoon, at dinner, and right before she went to bed. It equated to seventeen pills each day. I wondered just how effective all of that could possibly be, but our camp nurse assured me that to take her off the medication would do more significant damage in the long run. My medical knowledge is frightfully limited, but I had my doubts. How much worse could things get for Mindy?

One evening, a team leader frantically ran into the staff tent. Mindy was nowhere to be found. She loved the campfire time because it was her time to shine in the skits her team made up each evening. She was the star. Maybe because she could project her voice or maybe because her small frame was one of her most endearing qualities. Through those short evening dramas, Mindy was transported to a make-believe world where she could be anything she wanted. Often, when it was clear the skit was winding down, she would find a way to stretch it out until one of her team leaders said, "That's it!" or simply picked her up and carried her off the stage. It wasn't like her to abandon her team during evening activities.

Staff separated with the agreement to blow a whistle one long blast when she was found so we could call off the search. All the usually places were checked: other tipis, the ball field, the campfire circle, the arts and crafts area, and with acute fear, our pond and pool areas. Just about the time I was prepared to call an all-camp search, there was a piercing high-pitched sound, and we all ran in the whistle's direction. There was Mindy, lying slightly off one of the minor trails in camp, curled up in a near fetal position fast asleep. Waking her was not an option and she was carried to her tipi and tucked into her sleeping bag. I stayed with her until the campfire ended.

Watching Mindy sleep left me with so many questions. What unspeakable acts had she been forced to endure? How could one so small go through so much? What could I do to make a difference?

Mindy clung to her team leaders when it was time to climb in the van for the trip home. The thought of returning to yet another strange family must have weighed heavily on her mind. We hugged and there were promises of snow camps and Princess Clubs and many activities where we might just hang out.

She remained a part of TYM through middle school, but the real miracle in her life came with her last foster parent. She emphatically told Mindy, "You will be here until you want to leave. There is nothing you can do that will ever send you away." One amazing committed foster mom turned Mindy's upside down world right side up!

That God-like love – love without strings – allowed the healing process to begin. God's plan for His people is always to love without strings. Not just that overworked statement, "God loves you, and so do I." God-like love says, "I will roll up my sleeves and love you no matter what you do or what you say, no matter what the cost."

The last time I saw Mindy was a few weeks before her middle school graduation. Her foster mom was now her "real" mom. "After all, when you are adopted, doesn't that make you a real family?" she stated, more as a matter of fact than as a question. She was no longer taking any medication! Her mother and a sense of permanence had changed all that. And although at this point, college was not in her immediate future, she was thinking about going to a drama school. No surprise here.

THE BASEBALL CAP

As a ten-year-old, J is what some might call an *easy keeper*. He was willing to tackle any assignment, fun loving, and had a great laugh and even greater smile. He loved every aspect of camp, and participated enthusiastically in whatever was offered. It was hard not to like him. I only vaguely remember him, because he did not participate in any of the millions of camp fights that week – at least not to my knowledge.

It was the roughest camp in memory, and I left feeling a real sense of failure. We let the kids down. Not enough staff. Not enough *programs*. Not enough prayer. At the final campfire, several of the boys opened up to share a life of abject poverty, of witnessing too many shootings and murders and of severe neglect. One youngster queried, "I'm ten years old, and I love baseball. But my two-year-old sister calls me Daddy. I'm not sure what to do." Another had attended four relative funerals in the last six months – all senseless murders at the hands of gangs and guns.

Because of a number of moves, J did not return to camp until he was thirteen and went on a backpacking trip with fifteen other teens. It was a fairly uneventful five-days, no amazing feats of heroism or outstanding activities, but one adult – his team leader, Steve – formed a real bond with J during the trip. At the end of five days in the high Sierra, Steve made it clear that this was just the beginning of their long-term relationship.

It would take several books to chronicle all the things they did together: white water rafting, countless hours of tutoring, more backpacking trips, and many TYM outings and events. Eventually, Steve and his wife became J's godparents.

Several times, when Steve was not available, I served as a substitute teacher for J. He particularly had a hard time with basic math. While J could remember every football, basketball and baseball statistic, from batting averages and percentage of free throws made to receiving and running yards, it was the simple math that stumped him. It seemed curious that he struggled so hard to understand that two times three gave us the same answer as three times two. Using pennies to try to give J a physical image of the reasoning behind the math seemed to temporarily bring results. That newfound information had a very short-term effect on J. I started wondering if he had the smarts to even graduate from high school – until one day he told me his story.

"When I was maybe two, my real dad stole me, and we were on the run for the next few years. I remember my dad would send me into a store to steal food or money. I remember sleeping on park benches or empty cars and watching my dad do drugs.

"I think I was five or six when we were caught stealing hats from Sears. My dad went to jail and I went to live with a foster family. We were somewhere in the mid-west and it must have been several years before the police tracked down my real mom. I never stayed in any one place long enough to start school. Reunited with my mom, the school closest to where she lived decided to put me in fourth grade, probably because of my age and size. I knew I couldn't read or do any math or writing, so I got pretty good at being tough with other kids and charming with my teachers. I pretty much laughed my way through sixth grade.

"Of course, it got harder when I got to middle school and high school, but then my TYM family came into my life, and I felt I finally had a chance to catch up."

That changed my teaching perspective with J. He was definitely smart enough, but missing the beginning basics had certainly taken its toll. I often wondered why one of his teachers had not picked up on what was missing for all those years but were content to just pass him off to the next grade.

When J was sixteen, he asked and received permission to come and help out at a TYM boys' camp as a "Junior Team Leader." It was immediately evident that J had the really essential combination of qualities that would eventually mature into a very good team leader. And he wanted to serve, to do his part in giving back what was given to him.

J returned to serve as a team leader the following summer. Now seventeen, he was confident and observant in meeting the needs of his team. It was a good camp – few fights, very exciting activities and a challenging theme around expedition behavior. The boys really got it. If they work together with respect, they were able to do many things impossible to do by themselves.

J had a huge heart and cared deeply for hurting children, primarily because he remembered more difficult times in his own life. He loved to play with TYM campers and turn them into winners. He no longer had to let us all know just how good he was at swimming or playing basketball.

I can only imagine how difficult it was to let an eight-year-old, not yet skilled in shooting a basket let alone hitting the backboard, beat you in the game. J was a master at making that happen, without being too obvious.

On Saturday, as the campers were leaving, J was crying. They were tears of utter brokenness and a desire to have camp continue on forever.

On our drive home, J continued to cry, and I finally asked if there was anything I could do.

"It's Tim. I really love that kid. I hated to see him go home." I knew there was more to the story, and J continued.

"You know that first backpacking trip with Steve. I think I was kind of like Tim with Steve. We had such a great time together, and at the end of the trip, Steve told me we would stay in touch. He gave me his baseball cap as his pledge to me that he would stay in my life forever. And you know that has been true. You know all the stuff we have done together. Today, I gave Tim my baseball cap."

J got it! He recognized we are the richest when we pass on what has been given to us. Learn the lesson and pass it on!

J is now a college graduate and a church pastor. Whenever he has free time during the summer he joins our paid staff for a camp or two serving as a team leader, a basketball coach, and even directing several boys' camps. "You've always said that we need more black male role models at camp. Well, now you have one!"

I sometimes forget the depth and importance of role models and mentors from every ethnicity. Over many years I've observed thousands of kids at camp coming from less than ideal circumstances, and they are never just any one race. We'd love it if they were. Then I could rightfully say, "That's a white problem," and be a bit more dismissive. Although financially wealthy families of every background have a way of sweeping their less-than-ideal behaviors under the rug and have gotten pretty efficient at finding better ways to cover up their mistakes, abuse and neglect is most definitely an equal opportunity condition.

If we hope to move in that amazingly wonderful direction to be judged more on the content of our character than our financial or racial circumstances, (thanks to something Dr. King reminded us so many years ago) I believe our children will lead the way. From everything I have seen at camp, children really do care less about their individual differences and more about having fun together.

TAM – Today's Adults Matter!

I'm not sure why it took so long! It isn't that it was a brand new idea. God has been talking about family from the beginning. But TYM had a long history of working solely with children. That changed in late summer one year when seven moms and their nine TYM daughters arrived at camp on a Saturday morning. It was clearly long overdue.

They were excited, nervous and delighted – just like so many of our campers! Lunch was the first order of business, and after settling into tipis, we were off to the low ropes course. At first, the mothers were reluctant. Standing on a small wire on "Zigzag" looked difficult. The rules were given: "You must be touching a tree or touching someone who is touching a tree." There were three wires stretched less than a foot off the ground in a zigzag between four trees. The entire group had to go from the first tree to the last without falling off the wire and touching the ground. There was lots of falling off, and lots of laughter. Success only came when mothers figured out they needed to rely on their children's agility and their own willingness to fail. They all said afterward they learned something about teamwork and trust. Zigzag can never be completed alone.

The Wall presented yet another challenge. Boosting people up and over a twelve-foot wall is not easy. One mom told us later that she feared her weight would be too much for the rest of the team. At first, she stood back, not willing to risk certain failure. After several minutes of watching the rest of the group she spoke with confidence. "I may not make it to the top of the wall, but I can certainly help others get there." Not bad advice in any walk of life! Again, with success came confidence and a new level of trust.

We ate dinner together, and the mothers and their daughters performed songs and skits at the campfire. Four of the moms ate their very first s'more that night. If you do not know the messy joy when graham crackers, roasted marshmallows and chocolate squares collide, it maybe your time to try one! There were so many other firsts for the mothers: the first canoe ride, the first camping trip. But probably the thing they repeated over and over again, "We've never had a chance to play. You know, I never had a childhood. I've never had a chance to do things like this. When can we come back?"

In the morning, we flipped pancakes without spatulas – another first for all of them – memorized Matthew 6:21 ("For where your treasure is, there your heart will be also." NIV) and went in search of buried treasure. Each mom and daughter duo dug up a small box buried in a sandy spot near the pond to remind her that she is in fact God's treasure. God wants us to be very careful about picking the best for our lives.

We planned to paint each box for about fifteen minutes, enough time for most kids at camp to complete the project. The girls left the group to make bracelets for their mothers. The mothers refused to have any time limitations put on them. This was not going to be a quick paint job. They wanted their boxes to symbolize what they treasured and to make sure the outside looked as good as the inside.

And while the mothers continued to paint, they exploded with desire to share their personal stories of abandonment and subsequent abuse both while growing up and in adulthood. One lived under a bridge for nearly seven years. Another served time in prison for drug abuse. She laughed, "It took me a long time to realize, drugs and prison, prison and drugs. They go together!" Both women found the "One Step" program – Jesus – and began to live their new drug-free lives. One became *mom* to her six siblings at the age of ten, when their mother disappeared. When their daughters returned to give each mother a camp-made bracelet as a gift of love, the moms were deeply moved.

Toward the end of their weekend, we asked for words to describe their experience at camp. "Fun!" "Friendship," "Trust," "Love," "Teamwork." There was an overwhelming vote to get together again as mothers alone and mothers with daughters. We were encouraged to begin a mothers' Bible study and bring the Moms with their daughters to the snow together. One mother even suggested a TYM office slumber party. They had heard about our wonderful Princess Club room with all sorts of make-up and "dress-up clothes." I could only imagine the laughter and fashion show that would follow!

I'm not sure why it came as such a surprise to me how much we had in common. That weekend our differences no longer defined us but helped us to grow into something we all sought after. To the last person, they sought after becoming closer to others and closer to God and sprinkling it with a whole lot of love and laughter.

As we prepared to begin the journey back home, one mother said, "You should change the name from TYM to TAM. Because Today's Adults Matter, too!"

LOST

Twelve teen girls, four women, two men and four llamas; we left the parking lot in the Tahoe National Forest with two very seasoned guides who knew the area well. The llamas belonged to one of them.

One could write a dissertation on the pluses and minuses of llamas. Here are a few things that might be included:

- Their coats are extremely soft. If you are a teen girl, you are automatically drawn to touch.
- Llamas sometimes spit. You never quite know when it is about to happen, thus no prep time to turn and duck.
- Llamas can carry around seventy-five pounds. Overload one and he will simply lie down on the job.
- Maybe it is the way they look down on you, but they often are a bit intimidating. I always had the feeling they were telling me, "Just in case you want to know, I am better than you. Much better."
- The llamas on our trip were patient to a fault. Nothing rushed them.

Because there were only twelve girls, it gave us plenty of time to get to know each girl and what was on her mind. Mindy started a conversation within the first few yards from the trailhead. We learned she had several sex partners, she always carried protection with her just in case and she was hoping to catch her first fish in one of the lakes. We passed our first body of water – actually it was a very small, very shallow pond – less than a mile into the hike. Mindy begged to stop. It was only the skilled debater on our leadership team that convinced her the second or third lake would undoubtedly have bigger fish in it.

When Mindy actually did catch her first fish, it was trophy-size and worthy of hours of conversation about bait and how big it was. She measured and measured it again. The window of opportunity of actually eating it had long passed before she was ready to let go of her prize catch. It might have best served its purpose of giving Mindy a badly needed boost in her self-worth. We gave the unnamed fish a proper burial under a tree of her choosing where she promised to return to the site to pay homage.

While forming long-lasting relationships with our campers is critical, we never overlook the importance of presenting a clear easy-to-understand message of God's plan through Christ for our lives today and for eternity. Mindy was fascinated. She asked poignant questions about why God allows bad things to happen, how we know for sure that Jesus was talking to her and what God wanted for her in her lifetime. Mindy was carrying a whole lot of uncomfortably heavy baggage, and like so many of us, was not ready to let go of any of it.

Late one night, she tapped me on the shoulder and signaled me to leave the warmth of my sleeping bag, go outside of our tent and answer a few more pressing questions. I really did not want to mess up this opportunity.

Mindy looked at me straight on and asked, "If I accept Jesus – or God – in my life, will He make me give up sex?"

I knew my response mattered. I also knew she was hoping God would say unmarried sex was still okay. These are the moments I long for Jesus to show up and give one of those amazing answers he was so prone to do. This particular question has taken on many different forms with our TYM young people. Just substitute "drugs" or "cigarettes" or "lifestyle" for the word "sex." It was not unfamiliar territory.

I started at the beginning of my walk with Jesus. "Mindy, when I first became a Christ follower, there were many things I did I was not sure if God gave me His blessings to do. What I do know is that God 100% accepts us where we are with all our good and our not so good. Sometimes He helps us to see that some of our choices are not in our best interest. He even gives us the power to change our minds about how we feel about so many things. What you are doing today has nothing to do with accepting God's grace in your life."

My explanation did not come close to giving her the answer she wanted. "But are you saying that God will *not* make me give up sex if I accept Jesus?"

No matter how I framed the answer, Mindy wanted a *yes* or a *no* answer. Without that she was unwilling to take the chance. We went back in our tent with too many questions still hanging and one fourteen year old struggling in hopes God would sanction her established lifestyle behavior. As I drifted back to sleep, I realized how much Mindy and I were alike. I, too, had those conversations with God, desperately wanting to have my less than ideal behavior understood and sanctioned as okay. The minute I start down the path of, "I know you understand, Lord" or even "I know what your Word says, but ..." I am indeed in hot water.

The next day turned our trip on a new trajectory. We were spread out preparing to fish or swim or just relax around the lake for the morning when a helicopter flew repeatedly overhead. At one point it hovered within one hundred feet above our heads. Quite naturally, it made all of us a little nervous. One teen wondered if they were filming and maybe we all would get a royalty check for participating in an upcoming blockbuster. Another seemed nervous as if perhaps the police were after her.

Some of our questions were answered when two horseback riders came through to ask if we had seen a young boy in the area. It seemed he went missing the night before about ten miles from our campsite. Soon several volunteer search and rescue units came through asking the same question. Our twelve girls wanted to join in the search, but because of their age and what might happen if they stumbled across the missing youngster, we opted to stay together. We promised to make the emergency call on our satellite phone should he wander through our camping area.

It was clear that a child lost in the high Sierra wilderness was troubling to all of us. Around three thirty in the morning I was awakened by the guys letting me know they were joining the search at least until mid-day. They left with food, water, one llama and good flashlights and maps. We would stay put until they returned.

It was almost dinnertime when our two guides returned exhausted and a bit defeated. The youngster's whereabouts were still unknown, and it was looking more and more doubtful there would be a good ending to this story.

At the campfire, one of the men spoke to our campers from the heart. "This has been a difficult day for me. I really hoped for a positive outcome, but it is beginning to look as if that will not be the case. On our hike back from the search, I realized how much this is like our encounter with God. We can hide thinking no one will be able to find us, or we can chose to step out and shout, 'Here I am.'

I am pretty sure our lost boy would step out and shout if he could. But I want to say to all of you very precious young ladies God really wants you to say, 'Yes' to Him. Be available and open to His rescue. All the adults on this trip understand about how God has rescued them. I will be praying you will reach out and shout, 'Here I am' as well."

Mindy was listening to his words intently, and it seemed as if she wanted to say something. Instead of asking more questions, she withdrew from all conversations for the rest of our trip.

As with the lost child we later found out fell into a deep crevice and did not survive, some of our outcomes do not always have a positive ending. Mindy walked away from our trip unable to make a decision that might literally have saved her life.

The word *repent* has such a Biblical frame around it. It is reminiscent of Jonah and his admonition to the people living in Nineveh. But its meaning to feel sorry for what you have done and turn the corner in a healthier direction is so applicable today. That is what I often pray for our struggling children. I am certain the angels sing when anyone decides to *repent* and follow Jesus. But I have a hunch there is a special song and shout out when one of the least of these, against all odds, makes that life-altering decision. At least that is the way I hope it is.

PULL-UPS

Jonathan's caseworker had warned us in advance. She knew only part of his story. The "why" of it was still a mystery. After dozens of years working with abused children, one thing is clear. The minute you think you have "seen it all," the absolute worst of the worst, a child will arrive at camp with some unexpected baggage almost too unbearable for anyone to imagine.

For the past two years Jonathan refused to go in a bathroom. Any bathroom. The dozen or so therapists called in to review his case could only draw one conclusion. Some unspeakable act had happened in a bathroom somewhere. So Jonathan, age nine, wore Pull-Ups. For the first few hours at camp, it didn't seem to matter. He took them off during swim time – in the afternoon – so it wasn't until the early evening that other children began to complain. "He stinks." "He smells like pee." "And poop."

When his favorite team leader, Bob, pulled him aside and told him it was time to change his "Pull-Up," Jonathan fell apart. He screamed at his team leader and anyone within earshot, "I'm not wearing a diaper. I'm not wearing a diaper." It became his mantra throughout the week, and eventually, his team leaders rigged up a make shift shower close to their tipi, so he would not have to go very far to get cleaned up.

At times, his Pull-Ups were so urine-soaked, they hung well below his shorts. We all worried that he would develop some type of a rash – or worse. In our inability to make a difference, we found some consolation. After all, the "professionals" had known about his history for several years, and they couldn't figure out a way to break through.

Every day was a struggle. Wake up and change Pull-ups. A struggle. Change again mid-morning. A struggle. By the early evening, everyone on staff – Jonathan's team leaders and every adult at camp that week – was exhausted from the never-ending battle. We repeatedly tried to convince him to use the outhouse. That never worked.

On the third day of camp, Jonathan and Bob, the leader he liked most, almost came to blows. Jonathan began shouting obscenities and broke into uncontrollable sobs. "I'm not a baby. F – you. I'm not a baby. F – you!"

Now he was kicking and scratching, fighting what appeared to be the battle of his life. His second team leader sent a camper to find me. "Come quick. Jonathan is going crazy."

As I approached, Jonathan spilled out of the tipi on the run, barefoot, his diaper hanging well below his knee-length shorts. Bob was in close pursuit.

"Get away from me. Leave me alone. I hate you. I hate this camp. Get away from me."

Bob gently picked him up and cradled him in his strong arms, and Jonathan struggled as if his life depended upon it. Now, back inside the tipi, Jonathan was scratching and swearing and fighting to get loose with every ounce of strength he could muster. Bob kept cradling him and talking gently, "Calm down, Jonathan. It's going to be okay."

I am usually reluctant to blame Satan for bad behavior. When anyone attempts to tell me that, "Satan made me eat that extra donut," I want to scream, "It wasn't Satan. It was your lack of will power." Period. This was different. As the struggle continued, we looked at each other. We were certain that this was as close to "demon-possessed" as any of us had ever encountered. It was as if Jonathan had been taken over by Satan himself, and it was up to us to bind Satan on the spot.

While Bob continued to hold on to Jonathan, I began to pray, pleading with God to bind Satan from this place. Several other staff members, hearing the noise, came inside the tipi, and we joined hands to pray over this amazing child who seemed to be in the grips of Hell itself.

As we prayed, slowly Jonathan began to let go. Within minutes, the struggle was over, and Jonathan lay asleep in Bob's arms. They remained in that one spot for well over an hour.

It would be a bit of a stretch to say that Jonathan was a new camper after his ordeal. He continued to hate changing his Pull-ups, but he resigned himself to it several times each day.

On the last day of camp, just before our awards ceremony, Jonathan came up to me. Throwing his arms around my neck, he whispered in my ear, "I peed off the back of the tipi platform this morning."

I smiled broadly and told him how proud I was of him. There would be years of therapy and horrible memories in the future, but I sensed that Jonathan had turned a corner. Through the gentle persistent love of an adult who determined never to give up on this young man, Jonathan saw reason indeed for *Hope and a Future*. It is the promise to all of us. Surrounded by people wanting to make a difference, binding prayer and our Savior, we do not need to remain stuck in a spiral downward into the pit of hell. God's promise!

The Box Under the Bed

Snow is something only seen on television and in the movies for most inner city, vulnerable children. It looks fluffy – a mix between cotton candy and marshmallow paste. And it looks soft. It looks kind of like participating in a giant pillow fight.

The first patch of anything white – no matter that it is riddled with road dirt and tree branches and is less than two square feet in size – produces squeals of, "Stop! Let us out." It takes patience and great communication skills to convince a vanload of excited youngsters it is in their best interest to wait just a little longer with the promise that snow will get deeper, and it is always a lot more fun when there is more white stuff and fewer rocks on the ground.

Harriet let me know this was indeed her first trip to the snow. She was nervous. "What if I fall? I don't like to get too cold." Her fears of snowy conditions were not the only baggage she brought with her. Harriet was in the process of adjusting to yet another foster home, and she was fighting it every step of the way. It was just too difficult to listen to all those social workers grilling her about how she was adjusting and signing her up for more group therapy sessions. And then there was the new family feeding her that less-than-truthful line. "We are so glad you are here. Consider yourself one of the family." Only it always seemed to end when she wet the bed or pulled out her own hair or got upset over anything. Then the expected line would follow, "It's just not going to work out. You'll find a really good home. It is certainly not your fault."

Harriet often wondered why anyone in their right mind would believe that things would be any different in a new foster home. Her past was riddled with far too many broken promises masking a dysfunctional life.

Harriet settled into the expansive mountain dorm room and carefully unpacked her sparse belongings. In addition to one change of clothes, she placed her snow gear, given to every TYM child for use during the weekend, on the floor next to her bed. She was pretty happy when dinner was the next activity and she could postpone the inevitable slippery, freezing slip-n-slide outside.

A San Francisco Bay Area college church group was sponsoring the trip – covering all expenses and organizing some amazing, wild, and fun activities. They had taken great pains to plan each and every event with our children in mind. There were several fun games during dinner and lots of laughter. Did you know that with very little effort, you could make a spoon stick to your nose? Or play tunes with a simple straw? Or make milk shoot out of your nose? For a few hours, Harriet forgot about the disaster that she knew would be waiting for her when she returned from the trip.

There was a suggestion for some moonlight tubing, but some of the group was glad to stay in the lodge and play games – a huge relief for Harriet.

The next morning, Harriet stayed in bed as long as she could. She wandered down to the dining room moments before the family-style platters were carried back into the kitchen. Everyone was anxious to play outside, and I am sure Harriet was feeling no one would notice if she didn't join in on the first wave of inner-tubers.

It was close to mid-morning when I realized that Harriet was nowhere to be found. Preliminary checks of the meeting and dining rooms produced nothing. I was not quite ready to call in the posse so I continued to wander through the lodge. Finally in the corner of one of the dorm rooms, Harriet was sitting on the floor, knees close to her chest as she gently rocked back and forth hoping that she might remain invisible.

I sat down next to her saying nothing – close, but not too close. It is important never to touch abused children without permission, and it was clear that Harriet was not ready to give permission to anyone. We sat in silence for what seemed like hours, and finally Harriet spoke softly. "Why are you here with me and not outside having fun with everyone else?"

"Right now there is no place I would rather be than here with you." I sat quietly waiting for her response.

"I don't think I like the snow." And I asked if she had ever been to the snow before.

"No. But I don't think I will like it. Anyway, I've got a lot of stuff to think about." I knew that was a loaded response, and I decided not to press her to explain any further.

Harriet was ready to talk, and because I didn't press her to explain herself or seem anxious to get her outside, she began to let me into her troubled world.

Five foster families in less than three months. Taken from her home because of severe neglect and mom's drug dealing boyfriend in the house. Failing in school. (Is there any wonder with the lack of stability in her life?) No friends. Inability to trust anyone.

Harriet was spiraling downward as if in sheer free-fall, and I felt helpless to try to offer any answers to quell her rapid descent. I tried to imagine, even as an adult, if I were riddled with the dysfunction that surrounded her life, would I do any better? I could not imagine the pain she must be going through. It seemed completely unfair.

God, I am clueless what to say to this beautiful child of yours. Please give me the words of encouragement and relief – even if it is only a temporary fix.

To this day, I am not sure where this came from – unless it was a God-answered prayer.

"Harriet, I know you have gone through a lot of bad stuff. Most of it has nothing to do with you. But here we are right now in a very beautiful place with fresh snow all around us. I know you have great boots and ski pants. You can use my waterproof gloves. You will really be surprised at how much fun all the other kids are having.

"So here is what I want us to do. I have this great big box, and I want you to put all the bad stuff going on in your life in the box right now. We'll put really good tape around it and push it under your bed. When we get ready to leave, we'll get the box and you can bring it back with you. What do you think?"

Harriet's questioning smile turned to sheer glee as I pulled out a very large, imaginary box, and she carefully began putting "her stuff" into it. I'm not sure of the things she was selecting to go in the box, but she kept the loading process going, while I kept struggling under the weight of it all. Finally, she stood up and proclaimed everything she intended to include was there and that we could seal it up. We put the lid on the box, and with our imaginary duct tape, we sealed it tightly in every direction and then shoved it under her bed.

It was as if a huge weight had been lifted. I knew this was a temporary fix and that her life road would still be difficult. But for today – this one cold Saturday in the high Sierras of California – Harriet got a well-deserved break from the horror that was her life. We snagged some inner tubes and joined the others in downhill sled races and snowball fights, and more laughter than she had experienced perhaps in her entire life.

When the trip ended, Harriet was asleep in the van in a matter of minutes. Cold air and exercise has that effect on almost everyone spending a day in the snow. When we arrived at the parking lot where her foster parent was waiting to bring her home, Harriet did not protest. This had been a special weekend.

As their car began to pull out onto the street, it suddenly stopped and Harriet jumped out and raced toward me.

"We forgot the box. We left the box under the bed!"

She shrugged her shoulders and proclaimed softly as she climbed back into the car, "Oh well, we can get it the next time we go to the snow!"

abused children go
x foster to families

UGANDA – PART ONE

The faces were haunting. Most of the portraits were in black and white. A few showed smiles – most faces though just stared vacantly into an unfamiliar camera lens. The photos were on display at a local church during their mission faire. Photographer Blake Farrington had captured in the faces of those Ugandan children the plight of an AIDS epidemic gone wild.

We had just heard a great sermon about missions, followed by an array of cookies, hot and cold drinks and donuts of every size and shape. Standing in front of our TYM table, somehow I could not manage to shake those images. Were they orphans just trying to survive on hand outs until they reached adulthood and could make it on their own, or were they simply waiting for impending death? How many had lost parents, siblings and friends from the ravages of war and disease?

Years ago, I remembered seeing a commercial about AIDS, and well-known celebrities talked about the funerals they had attended in the past year. One had been to three. Another had attended seven. Then, an old African spoke softly about attending over three hundred funerals in the past year. God was not very subtle that day. He was speaking, and I had to make a conscious decision to listen or walk away.

So many verses popped into my head. "God so loved the world." Did that mean these children as well as those in my own backyard? "As you do unto the least of these, you do unto me." Was Jesus purposely trying to get my attention – to hit me with images I could not forget? This certainly wasn't going to be easy, but then, when does God ever call us to "easy?" This was a defining moment, one that visibly stirred my heart to get out of the comfortable and into a new adventure.

After all the years working in Christian camping with vulnerable children, the connection was just a little too obvious. The thought of running a Uganda camp for AIDS orphans had its beginnings that very moment. There were many meetings and even more correspondence with a Uganda program working almost exclusively with the ravages of AIDS and too many orphans. Finally, it was decided that a preliminary probing and planning trip would be in order.

There is probably nothing that could have prepared anyone from the United States of America for the sights, sounds and smells of Uganda. We arrived at the small airport near Kampala, the country's capitol, with a blast of "it's going to take a while to get used to this" heat. I discovered new sweat glands I previously believed only belonged to seriously ripped athletes. Something in the airport kitchen had caught on fire we were told, and the choking smoke permeated the entire baggage area. While waiting to get through customs and filling out a massive amount of paper work to claim a few pieces of luggage that didn't finish the journey with us, we took turns racing out into semi-fresh muggy air to grab a few deep breaths of anything except the airport's toxic smoke.

Joseph, a social worker with the program where we were partnering, greeted us. His English was perfect, and he was thoughtful, with subtle humor and grace. Joseph and his wife and three children were living with others either related or just in need. There were times when seventeen-plus individuals were under their roof often without personal financial support of any kind. Some were orphaned children. Others were broken families. It did not seem to matter their circumstances. They had a welcoming place to stay if there was a need.

His winning smile made me instantly feel at home. He had been assigned as my personal liaison to our upcoming camping program, and it was our job to work out all details and financial needs. He arrived with a small team of Ugandans and a large, old mini-sized bus – one I suspected had a bit of duct tape and bailing wire holding it together. They all spoke English and at least one other language. Our luggage, both personal and those filled with gifts for the Jinga-based ministry, was shoved through windows and back doors with just enough room for the variety of passengers including all of us from the United States and the Ugandan welcoming committee. We climbed between bags and boxes and settled in for a three-hour ride from Entebbe/Kampala to Bugombe – a small town a few miles from the outskirts of Jinja.

It was the most intense road trip I've experienced since barreling up a Costa Rican mountain highway on the wrong side of the road around a curve while passing slower vehicles. The Uganda road, mostly dirt with patches of pavement here and there, was covered with potholes, and our driver managed to miss about thirty percent of them. With each jarring bump, we might have been ejected were it not for our luggage wedged between airspace and us.

If you have traveled in a foreign country, you know about "round-abouts." They are intended to provide a way through a circular intersection whereby cars yield to other cars and traffic flows in an orderly fashion. They simply do not work that way in Kampala. At one round-about, cars were jammed at every angle, people hanging out of windows with small animals and children, so tightly squeezed every which way, I saw no way out. I had the feeling that only a miracle or a large crane could extract us from this mess, when, after about ten minutes, it loosened up, and we were on our way again.

The smell of burning plastic, animal waste and crowded streets defined our drive. Garbage collection simply did not exist. Huge randomly placed piles of refuse burned day and night, and the scent of burned plastic followed our bus the entire trip. People were everywhere carrying large bundles of wood and water on their heads or on their bicycles. One young man managed to balance a full-sized refrigerator on his one-speed bicycle – both prized possessions. I wondered if there were any power lines in his village.

As expected, the countryside was breathtaking. Everything was green, and Joseph pointed out a wide variety of birds and an occasional monkey. At one point, he motioned for the driver to pull over, and while vendors surrounded the bus, pushing their food through the open windows, hoping for a sale from a "muzungu" (their word for non-Africans), Joseph bought a small bunch of the sweetest bananas I have ever tasted. He warned us, "If you hope not to get sick, do not buy any food from street vendors unless you can peel it or bring it back for some serious cooking."

The village of Bugombe – our destination – was also filled with people. Some were attempting to sell something – from sticks for fires to food of every sort. Others were just walking. Children of every size and age were woven into the fabric of their daily life. They were always smiling, always wanting to grab a hand to walk with us even for a short distance. That physical connection was heartwarming. We were certainly foreigners but were immediately welcomed as honored guests of their community. It was never the fact that we were rich Americans. We were truly accepted.

I spent most of my time that week working on the hundreds of details to run a successful camp. Our "To Do" lists were long for both Joseph and me. It was important to make sure we did not forget anything. "It is not easy to run to the store for a forgotten item," Joseph warned. Most non-food camp supplies would come from the United States. Most personnel and all the food would come from Uganda.

Uganda – Part One

One day, Joseph was busy with his regular duties as a social worker. I spent part of that day visiting a local school, and they welcomed me warmly. The children in P-6 stood when I entered their classroom and sang a "Welcome to Africa" song for me. A tin roof made it impossible to teach over the noise from a brief pounding rainstorm. It was an open-sided room with dirt floors. There were no books – just a remarkable teacher and one blackboard. He asked me if I might like to talk to the children about life in the United States. Most understood English perfectly, but when words were introduced that would simply never come up in any Uganda conversation, their teacher tried his best to translate an equivalent word in their native Luganda language. I drew a rather poor map of Africa, and they knew exactly the location of Uganda. The children were patient as I struggled to finish the map of the rest of the world and particularly where I lived in California. Several older children knew of our then infamous "terminator" governor and asked if I had ever met him.

Somehow the conversation turned to what in particular I found different living in California from their beloved town. Thinking this might become a "teachable moment," I tried to explain recycling and picking up the garbage and trash that covered their small schoolyard. They nodded in unison when I suggested that we spend some time cleaning up around the school. Before we headed outside, one of the students asked me, "What do you do with your garbage in America?"

Looking back at what followed had to be a bit comical. I explained that every family in my city has three large plastic cans – with lids – different colors. The largest can – blue – we put in everything we hope can be recycled. Of course, they wanted to know what kind of stuff could be recycled, and I ran through the list my refuse company suggests to all its customers. The middle sized can – dark green – is for all the garbage. They haul it away and put it in the ground, cover it with dirt, and eventually, it becomes a golf course (which called for a whole different conversation) or a park or something beautiful. The smallest can is for garbage that can immediately be turned into mulch or compost. Their logic was way ahead of mine. "So what happens when your garbage cans are full?" Have you ever tried to explain something to someone that is completely out of his or her realm of understanding? No pictures. Just a very old blackboard, some chalk and a rather clumsy artist whose last art class was fifty years earlier.

"Well, there is this huge truck. With these long arms. That operates with a hydraulic lift." Oh boy, this wasn't working. I tried making my arms move just like I've seen them do on the garbage trucks. It was really ridiculous, and finally their kind teacher rescued me, saying something I could not understand. The class all smiled and nodded, and I suspected several wanted to laugh but were too polite to do anything that rude in front of me.

We all marched outside and in about a half-hour we picked up all the garbage and trash littering the schoolyard. They were so proud of themselves, and when I told them that burning plastic would be hazardous to their health, they agreed to bury everything that should not burn.

The school lunch, provided to all the children was the only real meal of their day. It consisted of posho (a cornmeal that is a staple food in Uganda), rice and beans and sometimes a little meat or fish. I understand that in some schools, children without a financial sponsor did not get to eat lunch, that in fact, even if they were hungry, they are physically removed from the lunch line. I was delighted this school fed all the children, no matter their circumstances. They ate with gratitude – for the food and for their ability to go to school while learning how to read and write.

The return from school to the walled compound I called home during my stay took me past a number of small shacks, a public outhouse and hundreds of children some too young for school; others with family responsibilities that left them supervising younger siblings. The dirt roads in Bugumbe were red and badly rutted from the ravages of the rainy season. The minute I started walking, children from everywhere ran toward me hoping to grab one hand or request some of the bottled water I usually carried with me. I was told never to give my water to anyone. It would start something in the village that would have been hard to contain. I felt humbled and blessed to be in the presence of such smiling, happy children. In spite of their dire circumstances, they found reason to laugh and dance and sing.

I made a mental note to myself to try to be more grateful for the abundance that becomes daily routine in California.

One morning, before the sun rose high enough to melt everything in its path, I got up and decided to take a pre-breakfast walk. Unlike local residents, Americans were fed well. I knew that an abundance of coffee, pineapple, toasts, cereal, eggs and some meat would be waiting when I returned. There was a circular hike behind our compound that offered a majestic view for miles with a promise that I would probably be able to negotiate the streets back to my starting point. Already, many of the villagers were up and about, going to the market or hauling water from the town well. Under the age of three, children carried quart size bottle. By the time you were ten, you were expected to carry a full five-gallon container.

Suddenly I became aware of someone behind me. My first instinct was to run. I surely was not ready to die in the jaws of a lion that must have been stalking my every step. As I turned I was greeted by one of the girls I had met in P-6 the day before. She smiled broadly and stated, "Good morning, Miss Marilyn. How are you?" Before I had a chance to respond, she broke the slice of bread she was carrying in half and offered it to me. I stumbled through something about breakfast waiting for me back at the compound, but I was truly shaken by her gesture. This young lady was willing to share her one slice of bread with me. I was fairly certain that it was all she had to eat since her school lunch from the previous day. I felt too fat, too rich, too privileged and way too American.

With the camp ready to go in three months, we left Uganda feeling quite ready to experience our first African camp for vulnerable children. The real adventure was about to begin!

Uganda – Part Two

Those three months whizzed by. There were many emails flying back and forth between Uganda and the United States, and everyone was on the same page as to what needed to be done in both countries to insure a successful inaugural camp. Packing everything we would need to run back-to-back camps for Ugandan girls was a far greater challenge than we anticipated. We were seven seasoned camp staff members – all familiar with TYM and our work with vulnerable children. We were also aware that certain camping items would simply not be available once we arrived in Uganda. Everything – or so we thought – needed for camp was tightly packaged in large plastic tubs, carefully weighed and securely tied for our long journey.

There was one pretty awkward moment when we tried to bring a slightly used chainsaw with miniscule traces of gasoline onto the plane. (After all, it *was* in the luggage compartment wrapped tightly in one of the tubs.) It simply never occurred to us that our airline would not understand how difficult it would be to find a workable chainsaw in Uganda and let it slide. Today, an arrest would most likely be in order. (There was one awkward moment I am told when a TYM friend went to retrieve the chainsaw from the airline and ended up with an escort to her car!)

Our reception when we arrived in Kampala/Entebbe was warm and gracious. The entire Uganda adult camp team greeted us at the airport, and we instantly sensed this would be an amazing few weeks. Joseph had done everything on his "to do" list prior to our arrival. The three big non-food items – mosquito netting, mattresses and blankets – had already been loaded on our three boats and were heading to the far shore of Lake Victoria where the camp was to be held. The food would be brought in daily to insure freshness.

There are several advantages of camping on Lake Victoria – and a few disadvantages. Uganda heat is sometimes unbearable. By noon, even the shade of one of their many trees offers little relief. But by two in the afternoon, the lake breeze picks up, and the temperature drops significantly.

On the downside, the combination of heat and breeze causes millions of small green unnamed insects to swarm into camp. They hover around until after dark when the attraction of nightlights brings out the worst in them. They are thick and annoying, flying into face and body indiscriminately. There is no escape except to slink into a really dark corner where insects rarely venture.

Staff training lasted for the better part of two days. The Uganda team was most anxious to learn everything we knew about camping and kids, although I suspected there would be more than a few unexpected challenges. The women all wore skirts. I wondered how they would actively participate in a rousing soccer or volleyball game. Would they tuck their skirts above their knees and hope for the best? The author of that old adage "necessity is the mother of invention" must have had these energetic women in mind. They were ferocious in attacking every challenge presented.

The Uganda team spoke several languages and dialects. Our USA team felt a bit inadequate. Most of us knew but a few words beyond our own English. We decided well before arriving in Uganda that our USA group needed to take our lead from those knowing the children and the language. We had no idea what a remarkably brilliant idea that would be.

Joseph left early one morning and arrived by boat in the early afternoon with forty-two girls. Some were so excited they could hardly contain their joy and laughter. Some had a "deer in the headlights" look – one that said, "I'm close to panic, but I may be willing to stick it out for at least a few days." The Uganda camp team burst into song and dance with words I could only imagine. Those of us from the United States tried to dance and hum and look as if we truly were a part of all this, but I am sure the girls had their doubts. It was all a little awkward.

In those two weeks of camp, there were deep learning lessons for all of us.

Uganda girls care less about the win than they do about everyone participating. During every activity – from a simple run and chase game to a heated soccer match – they all jump up and down with joy for all the teams, no matter what their order of finishing or who scored a goal.

Ugandans are polite and service oriented. Throughout the entire camp experience, the minute I stopped eating after any meal, a camper immediately grabbed my plate to bring it from the table to the dishwashing area. There seemed to be a genuine appreciation of our effort to bring a United States camping program to Uganda, and they made sure we knew the experience was one they would never forget.

One of the local chickens liked our camping area enough to hop through a glassless window and lay her one daily egg on one of the cots. After several days, we decided to collect the eggs until we had enough for an egg toss game. Children would stand opposite their partner and toss an egg back and forth until it was either dropped or broken. We were preparing to begin the collection process when one of our campers was spotted walking over to the bed and carefully wrapping the chicken's daily gift in a tissue to bring home with her. Our plans changed immediately. The game we played so many times at camp in the United States without a thought of our wastefulness suddenly stood as a stark reminder of doing our part in their fight for survival.

Ugandans can sing – on key, in at least three-part harmony, no matter what the circumstances. And they can dance – with rhythm, to the beat, all the time, for hours at a time.

Uganda girls would rather bring home their brand new shorts, shirts and camp shoes than actually wear them at camp.

And at the first sign of dirt anywhere on anything they might call apparel, washing shoes and clothes becomes the primary activity of the day. (I wanted to transport several girls to a California TYM camp and teach our own campers this type of behavior.)

Few Ugandan campers could swim. But they love the water and could have spent hours in warm Lake Victoria. Jumping up and down in the lake was enough. Because of sharp rocks and broken bottles in the water, it took a lot of pleading to get them to wear shoes.

Girls from northern Uganda suffered deeply from the after-effects of so many years of war, rape and destruction. They had lost their ability to smile. The magic of camp served as a brief respite from the horrors back home. I thought I had some understanding of just how devastating The Lord's Army had been on the Uganda people. I left Uganda realizing again the truth to that statement, "The further you are from the frontlines, the more you are likely to believe that everything is all okay."

One morning I decided to get up around 5 a.m. to have some "God and me" time. The Ugandan adult team had been awake since before 4 a.m. I watched from a comfortable distance as individually they petitioned God on behalf of all campers and their country and continent at large – all done with praise and thanksgiving for life itself. Without benefit of any flashlight or lantern they walked and prayed. I did not see any signal or call, but around 5:30 they pulled together to pray and praise corporately. God was indeed their clear salvation. He is the

only answer in a country dying from the ravages of civil war, the Lord's Army and AIDS.

The two weeks went by a little too quickly for my liking. I left with a new understanding of the importance to remember how much "stuff" I actually have and always to have a grateful heart – and then try to live on a whole lot less.

No matter what my circumstances, I always want to be in a position to proclaim, "All this and salvation, too!"

BRANDI

Every once in a while, a child leaves an indelible imprint, simply impossible to forget. Sometimes it's a certain look. Often there are a few words spoken that change everything. Whatever that specific thing is, we are all changed because of it.

When Brandi cautiously stepped out of the car transporting her to camp, the other campers flocked around her immediately. They sensed the same thing every adult recognized. She was special.

Already, at age nine, she was stunningly beautiful with dark brown, dancing eyes that perfectly matched her thick, shiny, brown hair.

She was instantly everyone's best friend and the center of anyone of the six teams of her choosing. When teams were picked, she was surrounded and finally settled on the team that seemed to "will" her to join them. Her new teammates all wanted to carry her small duffle bag to their assigned tipi several hundred yards across the dusty field. It was undoubtedly new to her to be courted like this. Her background put her at the bottom of her foster family line-up. Brandi looked bewildered, not quite sure what to make of all the attention.

I watched as she followed her team to their home for the week – the fourth tipi on the left. Two of her teammates walked on either side of her, grabbing her hands as if they were appointed to be her new best friends and caretakers.

They were inside their new home for only a few minutes when Brandi's five teammates spilled out into the open shrieking, "She's got lice." "Get her away from me. Get her away."

The nurse was summoned, and Brandi was marched across the field military style until she came to a halt directly in front of us. The nurse smiled politely and said, "Now, let me take a look."

I had seen the drill before. As a former teacher, I knew how to look for the tenacious eggs attached to each strand of hair. I had watched the school nurse blow gently through a straw to separate the hair so that nothing would slip by unnoticed. That type of detailed attention was not necessary with Brandi.

The lice were everywhere. Still attached eggs. In the just hatched nymph stage. Fully-grown active and crawling lice (about the size of a sesame seed) ready to reproduce. The camp nurse shook her head slowly, turned toward me and whispered loudly enough for Brandi to hear, "She's got to go home for treatment."

To this day, I am not sure how this could have happen, but I completely lost this little, frightened, beautiful child and only saw the lice. I held her at arm's length and tried to be as caring as possible – at a safe distance. Quietly hoping I could take the vehicle with the plastic seats, I drove her home. Except for the phone call to make sure there would be someone to greet her when she arrived at her home, not one word was spoken.

Even as a relatively new Christian, I had been put to my first test – my Peter denying Jesus moment – and had failed miserably. Somehow, I couldn't shake the thought of all those wretched tiny lice. A scared little girl was looking for some assurance that it would all end up okay. For the price of a bottle of lice shampoo, I could have hugged and reassured her that our camp would always be there for her.

Caught between what Jesus would have done and my own miserable reality, I had taken the path that would cause me the least discomfort.

It would be years before the whole ordeal was put into perspective. I was attending a small group Bible study, and we were confessing our deepest personal failures. All of us had committed what we knew were really big failures – different from everyone else's minor infractions. We ended the study with that horrible night when both Judas and Peter betrayed and denied Jesus. Both felt absolutely horrible about the events of the day and evening. But the two moved in quite different directions once that reality hit them.

Judas was completely loved (didn't Jesus called him 'friend'?) but he simply could not shake what he had done. Judas saw no hope. Peter walked away from his mistake and started the church! It is not our mess-ups that define us as much as what we do with them afterwards. Thank you, Peter, for giving people like me hope for forgiveness and still yet another fresh start.

Mud on Your Face

The steep hill from the camp's pond to the road below was a perfect setting for a makeshift water slide. All it took was a layer of hay spread over the shallow depression from the top of the hill to its base. Then it was covered with a thick black plastic tarp. The landing was sometimes a bit rough. Although great effort was taken to remove the millions of tiny rocks beneath, it did not always work out as planned. There were more than a few "ouch" and "ooohs" as rocks and small bottoms collided.

At the end of the run there was a small makeshift pool. As the children flew down the hill – with soap and water guaranteeing a fast track – they came to a rather abrupt halt in a large puddle of water. Of course, before long water and loose dirt combined to make a really muddy mess.

The only direct path to the swimming pool from our tipi village led right past the oozing thick goop. One youngster walking with her team leader stumbled right into it. She looked with anguish as her once clean white shoes turned into a soupy brown slime.

She began to cry. "My mother is going to kill me. My good shoes – all yucky. What am I going to do?"

Her team leader did not miss a beat. "We can get the mud off your shoes. Do you know that some people pay large sums of money to get mud facials." There was that incredulous look that screamed, "Say what?"

Her team leader continued. "You have to go to an expensive spa to get mud like this. People train for years to work in a spa like that!"

The tears stopped and the incident past almost unnoticed.

Unnoticed until half the campers showed up with mud smeared on their faces. They had taken to heart the encouraging words of a team leader and turned small tragedy into magnificent triumph.

It Pays to Keep Promises

Selena really did not want to go to camp. She was pretty sure she would not make any friends, and camp would probably have too many mosquitoes and bugs, and way too much dust and dirt. But her caseworker insisted, and Selena discovered the joy of learning to swim and canoe. She particularly loved watching stars and asked questions rarely posed by any child her age. By the time her camp ended, Selena pressed for an answer to that all-too-familiar question, "What's next?"

Her sixth grade teacher called me in late September. "Selena simply will not stop talking about her summer camp experience. She cannot wait for your fall programs to begin. Maybe you can help because right about now, we are not sure what to do to keep her in school." She explained that if someone did not intervene soon, Selena most likely would become another school dropout statistic. She was failing in school. She would fail to show up in the morning; fail to do any homework; fail to keep from fighting for almost any reason and fail to treat teachers with any respect. The school was giving up on her. It took way too much energy to keep her in the classroom. Her teachers were exhausted, and who could blame them. Often they spent as much time each day with Selena as they did with the rest of her classmates.

So together we worked out a plan whereby her teacher would measure some very specific behaviors (getting to school on time; in her seat; with two sharpened pencils; homework done), and when Selena completed all her assignments over a two-week period, I would take her out of school for an overnight adventure.

Almost instantly, Selena blossomed. Our adventures were of her choosing, and we went to the coast, to the mountains and to the movies. During one of our trips, Selena began to tell me her story. An older brother raped her when she was five. By the time she was eight years of age, she had been involved incestuously with a stepfather, an uncle and her grandfather, and it continued over a three-year period.

Finally, a neighbor blew the whistle on the family, and a caseworker was assigned to her. Selena was placed into the foster care system and lived in seven different homes over the next two-year period. Eventually, custody was given to an aunt who lived in a very small mobile home in her town. Selena's bedroom had just enough space for her small bed and a two-drawer dresser. Lying on her bed, she could touch opposing walls with bent elbows.

Then the totally unexpected happened. A young woman was trying to win a local beauty contest, and she needed to show her more compassionate side. Somehow, she convinced Children's Protection Services to let her take a "child in need" out for a Coke after school. Selena was selected. She was beyond excited. This would be her moment to shine. Her aunt bought her a new flowered shirt, and she was even allowed to wear lipstick to school. For one of the first times in her life, Selena felt "pretty" and ready for her new status as the center of attention.

The event went off without a hitch. Pictures were taken. A stuffed bear holding a red heart was given, and Selena could not contain her deep joy. The young woman gave her a hug with the promise,

"We'll get together again real soon. I'll call you." And for the next six months, Selena raced home to sit by the telephone for that call that would never come.

The look of deep sadness in her eyes as she relayed this story made clear the importance of promises kept. I am certain the simple words, "I'll call you" were not made lightly. The young woman's intentions were probably honorable. But after leaving Selena, other priorities pressed in, and her quest for fame took over her life leaving a shattered, disappointed twelve year old in her wake.

Often when sexual abuse occurs, a young girl will move in one of two directions. Either she will become tough – Selena tough – so that no one will ever touch or challenge her again. And she will likely put on weight – sometimes a lot of weight. Or she might become a wallflower – with an attitude that if I fade into the background, eventually no one will notice that I am even here. Either way, the price is way too high.

I believe that if Christians had any idea of the catastrophic devastation that sexual abuse inflicts upon the innocent, we would stand up in unison and declare, "Enough!" And then we would follow through with whatever it takes to put teeth into our proclamation. It simply is not enough to say we will pray for our vulnerable children or even that we will throw money at the problem. There has to be more.

The seeds of abuse begin far earlier than we would like to believe. Sometimes they begin even before a child is born.

Recently I watched an on-line preview of the film "Voiceless" about the Church standing up for the unborn children of the world.

And stand up we should. Ending a life before it has a chance to begin is clearly not part of God's plan. The church puts immense energy, thought, and purse into the fight for the unborn child. Massive efforts are undertaken to battle against abortion as a means of birth control, although when interviewing women and girls who live through the ordeal, few actually do so with a casual "Oh, well" attitude. Often it is viewed as the only viable option. It is not hard to feel empathy toward the thirteen-year-old girl, confused and scared at her choices over the next nine months and perhaps the rest of her life when rape or incest brought her to this place.

Although the issue of legal abortion is fraught with protest, anger, and intense debate, what bothers me deeply is that our love and concern – and may I say the stance we take – tends to disappear at that moment of birth. When decisions having to do with the nurturing and raising of that very child we wanted to keep alive in the womb, we far too often are simply absent. Our responsibility appears to end at the moment an infant takes his first breath.

I am gratefully aware that recent efforts – often encouraged by hands-on churches – to stay involved in each precious life has made a huge surge. What would happen if those efforts were duplicated one hundred-fold nation-wide?

What if we felt the passion for the unborn child for the rest of his or her natural life? What would that look like? If that passion remained alive, would we look at the death penalty differently? Would we be compelled to put an end once-and-for-all to the ghetto where she was forced to grow? Would we care deeply that college or trade school was an opportunity for that fetus we fought so hard to protect?

This audacious, crazy, out-of-control walk with Jesus may I suggest asks – perhaps even demands – we carry our commitment to the unborn over an entire lifetime. What would happen to all of us in the process?

- Maybe we would buy groceries for momma so she would not have to sell her body to afford feeding and housing that child we made sure would come into this world.
- Maybe the pull of selling drugs to make a fast buck or to escape from the pain of day-to-day living would be diminished by the knowledge that if we work hard there

would be someone in our corner to serve as an encourager and friend.
- Maybe we would come to understand what it really means to walk in the dust of the rabbi.
- Maybe many of the problems of guns and violence would be diminished by the sheer weight of our love.

Years ago, Rebecca Pippert wrote a book entitled *Out of the Saltshaker and into the World*. It was a best seller beyond just the Christian community. It reminded us of God's plan to no longer be content to be the salt of the earth by remaining in the bottle.

I can only imagine!

Sally Salamander

Kendra spent most of her non-school hours in her bedroom. Friends were really hard to find and even harder to keep. It was so much easier to simply avoid social situations once the school day ended.

When Kendra was eleven, she was referred to TYM with the thought she might benefit from a week at summer camp with girls her own age. She reluctantly consented.

Camp was hard. Too many people. No television. And all those strangers. Kendra kept to herself. She only participated in the eating, sleeping and swimming activities – all favorites. Until the afternoon on the second day.

Our camp developer/maintenance/general I-can-do-it-all person had just emptied a load of firewood and now was cleaning out the back of his pickup as Kendra was walking by. "Kendra. Come over here. I want to show you something." Her eyes darted to where he was standing in the truck. As she awkwardly climbed into the truck bed, she glanced around and probably would have bolted... until she noticed the most beautiful sight she had seen at camp – a really tiny salamander. She was mesmerized. It was slender from tip-of-nose to tip-of-tail.

Of course, salamanders do not move all that fast. Kendra opened a flat hand to receive the gift.

It was love at first sight. "Can I keep it?" she queried. A nod of approval was all that she needed. She carefully slid out of the truck and came looking for me. "Marilyn, do you have something I can put my salamander in? I've already named her. She's Sally. Sally Salamander."

We found a plastic aquarium in the back of the tool shed, filled it with leaves, a few small rocks and a little wading pool. Sally now settled into her new home. Kendra brought Sally to every camp activity. Swimming, dinner, the ropes course or a volleyball game. It didn't matter. Sally quietly watched every activity without protest.

Kendra tried taking Sally out of her small home at night so that they might share a sleeping bag, but she soon figured out that Sally would eventually dry out, causing her ultimate demise, or she would have to remain in her habitat – close-by – within a few feet of the sleeping bag. The rest of the campers and leaders sharing the tipi grew rather fond of Sally. She became their mascot – their very quiet mascot. They all caught as many mosquitoes as possible – not a difficult task at camp. No one ever saw Sally eat, but they were sure she did. After all, she did not appear to be losing weight.

On the last day of camp, I gave the "Salamanders can not live for very long in a cage" speech. I think Kendra knew deep down that it was right. Without protest, she carefully picked up Sally and carried her new best friend to a small nearby stream.

She gently kissed Sally on the nose instructing her to "Have a good life," and Sally disappeared into the gentle current. No tears. Just a sincere wish for the best possible life. As it should be with all of us!

Lizardbeth

One summer, TYM – without a camp of our own – rented a small Boy Scout camp about an hour's drive from where our campers lived. It was dreadfully hot all summer making the near Olympic-size pool the highlight for swimmers and non-swimmers alike. Sometimes when temperatures soared, pool-time began shortly after breakfast, and with a brief break for lunch, ended right before dinner. We went through giant bottles of sunscreen, and 100% of our campers learned how to swim!

As expected, there were thousands of Western Fence lizards reluctantly willing to be caught – and more than happy to be released. Campers often begged to take them home. It led to great discussions about our environment and looking, maybe catching, but always releasing. The lizards were everywhere, and on occasion they found their way inside one of our six tipis. (Actually so did several tarantulas, but that is an entirely different story!)

Just before swim time mid-week, three girls from Tipi #3 came running up to me protesting loudly, "There's a lizard in our tipi! Help us! What should we do?"

Unlike Alligator lizards that can bite, Western Fence lizards are docile and fairly easy to catch, particularly when they are over or under heated. I questioned them enough as to size, color and shape to determine it was indeed not an alligator lizard. Then I responded to their initial cry for help. "She probably wandered into your tipi and simply did not know how to get out. You will be able to catch her fairly easily. And if you turn her over and gently rub her tummy, she will love it."

Slowly they trekked back to their tipi, holding hands as if to declare, "The three of us can take you down, lizard, so don't try anything funny."

About an hour later they skipped up to me all smiles. "You were right. She just wanted to get out of the tipi. And she loved having her tummy rubbed. We let her go in the garden so she could have food to eat and some shade and water at the same time. Before we let her go we named her. Her name is Elizardbeth!"

I Got Your Back

Most of the children coming to camp live in the greater San Francisco Bay Area. For our own transportation convenience and the chance campers will stay in touch with each other, we further divide our children by local counties. Of course, there are always exceptions to the rule.

Tracy was one of those exceptions. She was born in a difficult community where drugs and shootings infiltrated her life for as long as she could remember. At camp she mused what life might have been like if her family structure had been different.

"All my family is either in prison or they're dead. You know drugs will do that."

Tracy eventually left the San Francisco Bay area and moved around the entire state of California with a variety of relatives including several cousins, grandparents on both sides and a few distant family friends. The State finally stepped in just before her eighth birthday, and she was placed into the foster care system. Six foster homes later and more case workers than she could remember, Tracy was moved to the outskirts of Sacramento, almost two hours from the Bay Area. It was defined a desperation move – a last resort.

No one seemed capable of putting in the time and effort it would take to stop her spiral downward. That is until she moved in with her new miracle-working family! Her most recent caseworker knew this amazing family and their ability to love desperate children into a positive direction of hope for their future. But they had rules that defied normal foster care standards. Foster children would be expected to attend church as a family. They would all eat meals together. This was a child's last stop. They would never send one of *their* children to yet another foster home.

Those commitments gave Tracy the stability she longed for since early memory, and she began to blossom. Make no mistake. This was no easy fix. But might I suggest that unconditional love and the actions that compel and drive our every love action is the only long-lasting answer to help an entire population of struggling children. Anything less is simply the "Band-Aid" option. If we cover enough wounds, we will not need to see and thus deal with the underlying problems. Those "problems" left untouched will surely fester and bring down a whole generation of young people.

Tracy's new family knew of our camp as they had sent other children in the past. Camp was a natural building block for Tracy to take. Her foster mom drove the three plus hours to get her to the campsite. When they stepped out of the car together, Tracy was ready to go. She ran over to her "mom," kissed her on the check and said, "You're coming back to get me at the end of camp. Right?" Knowing her past history of neglect and abandonment and way too many caseworkers, the answer came back with a laugh and an emphatic, "Yes. You bet I'll be here."

That answer spoke loud and clear. It is much the same as the ageless game of peek-a-boo we play with our very small children. It takes time and practice for a child to fully understand that the blanket over my head does not remove me from the presence of the one playing the game. It is reasonable to feel that assurance, but it takes time. Tracy was playing the peek-a-boo game. If you disappear out of sight, will you still be there after the game is over? And she received the thumbs up most children her age have long ago outgrown.

After a number of years of study, there has been much written about the value of pairing foster children in homes that share some of the same ethnicity as the children they serve. I have heard youngsters tell me they have, as they put it, "lost" the language of their origin. They always have a sense of sadness in their voices. It is almost as if they have been forced to abandon part of themselves. Many of us who cannot easily identify our entire ancestral roots tend to be a bit dismissive as to its importance. I am not sure I am prepared to keep up with my German, French, Polish, English, Russian and a variety of other languages yet to be disclosed!

While I personally would never want any child to put aside all the history that went into making him or her who they are, there is a bit more to this complicated puzzle. And Tracy's new mom was as sensitive to their racial differences as anyone I have ever met. She honored the fact of their different skin color while protecting Tracy from her less-than-ideal past. She was a walking reminder of Colossians 3:12-14, "Therefore, as God's chosen people, holy and dearly loved, clothe yourselves with compassion, kindness, humility, gentleness and patience. Bear with each other and forgive whatever grievances you may have against one another. Forgive as the Lord forgave you. And over all these virtues, put on love, which binds them all together in perfect unity." (NIV)

It did not take long for Tracy to embrace living with a predominantly black family. She told me during our week together, "Mom is teaching me how to cook all that yummy southern food." I pressed her for her favorite meal that if needed we could duplicate at camp – with her help. It turned out that eating three meals a day with abundant healthy snacks was a new concept for Tracy. Most often she had learned how to fend for herself when she was hungry. Finally, memories of hungrier days were beginning to fade.

Living with freckles – lots of freckles – and very white skin took some adjusting at camp. Tracy was the sunscreen application target of multiple staff members. Eventually she learned not to protest and just accept yet another layer of that white stuff lavishly slathered all over her body.

By mid-week, Tracy seemed quiet and withdrawn. It was clear something was wrong. It could have been a touch of homesickness. It might have come from just an overwhelming number of nonstop activities. Several on staff tried to talk with her, but she was having none of it. I guessed it might have come from a few too many people prodding her with questions for as long as she could remember. We corporately decided to walk alongside her without any more questions.

Quite unexpectedly at one of our nightly campfires, Tracy decided it was time to talk. She interrupted our crazy songs and off-the-cuff skits and immediately had our attention.

"You all know, I don't live near any of you. I've been moved all over place for as long as I can remember. I never met my real dad, although when I was really young, there were lots of guys around. Most of them did a lot of drugs, and I think they are all dead or in prison. My real mom left me with my aunt when I was two months old. I never met her either."

All of our campers were leaning into what she was saying. Maybe it was hitting too close to home. Several started crying softly. Tracy continued, "I'm living near Sacramento with a really cool family. The lady that drove me to camp is my new mom. I call her mom, because she is the first person I have met that I really wish were my real mom. She really likes me.

"Where we live I am the only white kid in the entire school. Some of the kids there like to fight, and I guess I am usually the one they want to fight with. So I just stay by myself most of the time. For the last couple of days, I realize I am the only white camper here. And it sometimes makes me kind of nervous."

Dee was sitting directly behind Tracy as she spilled out her story, and she reached over to touch her shoulder and gave words of assurance. "Don't worry, Tracy. I got your back."

It was a perfect response – something we all long to hear. Dee was a confident camper, respected as a leader. When she made a proclamation, you could take it to the bank. Tracy leapt from her bench and hugged Dee warmly. And Tracy was once again one of us. Ready to take on the world, knowing she had someone in her corner should the need arise. Tracy was longing for this kind of support, and it came perfectly wrapped in love and acceptance.

I've (We've) got your back! They are simple words shouting to all of us. When life takes an unexpected turn, I've got your back. When drugs, alcohol and gangs are pushing you into something and you are not sure about the end results, we've got your back. And might I say, when your church is taking a new turn and you might wonder where it will eventually lead, Jesus is saying to all of us, "Don't worry, Church. I've got your back."

Touch That Dial

Kay was one of twelve teen girls in our group, and we all got along well. Although there was from time to time a budding disagreement bordering on escalating into an out-of-control knockdown fight, for the most part everyone in the group knew that if the excursions were to continue, they had to do their part to make it as pleasant as possible for all the adults.

One of many camping trips to the snow had been well planned. We were going to drive to Diamond Lake – an easy drive from the Rogue Valley in southern Oregon. Although there was a huge lodge in operation year-round, we would find a deserted road close by, yet still unplowed, drive as far as we could and then walk a short distance to a fairly flat place to put up the fourteen by sixteen foot tent, big enough to comfortably sleep our group. We brought along an expert – our program's executive director Jack Smith with years of snow camping experience. He would help get us to our destination, put up the tent, carry in and attach the wood stove and then retreat to the safety of his own tent but close enough to come to our rescue should trouble erupt. I suppose the thought of sleeping in the same tent with twelve giggling teen girls did not have a huge appeal, but he was more than happy to help out and serve as our bodyguard from a distance. The girls knew and respected him and were willing to postpone inner tubing, snowball fighting and relaxing until the tent and all our supplies were in place.

The pole tent went up quickly. Lashed between two trees and the sides secured with mounds of snow, we thought we would surely be safe against any weather conditions thrown our way. The tent stove was quickly put into place. It rested on two logs in the snow and within minutes the stove fire was blazing. We scattered a bale of hay and placed a huge tarp over the hay, separating us from the cold snow. We were soon warm and ready to face the elements.

There was a great inner tube run directly behind the tent. It seemed completely out of character watching teenage girls – tough and street smart by most standards – rolling in the snow, making snow angels, throwing snowballs and laughing so hard several complained they had "peed in their pants."

Suddenly we looked up to see smoke billowing out of the tent. Jack raced inside, followed closely by a line of teens to discover that the two logs separating the stove from the snow had caught on fire. Jack immediately pulled the logs from under the stove and threw them outside. The impending tent fire disaster was averted for the moment, but now a very hot stove sat directly on the snow. Even high school physics dropouts could predict the inevitable. Slowly our stove melted the snow surrounding it and began its descent until it came to rest on terra firma, about four feet below. The stovepipe, at one time sticking a good five feet above the ceiling of the tent now barely poked out above the roofline. Without missing a beat, Jack built a small barricade to keep the girls from falling on top of the stove into the deep ravine it had created.

It did not seem to affect the function of the stove. The tent stayed warm and cozy, as long as we kept adding fuel. Even when the stove was filled to capacity with fresh dry wood, the girls repeatedly reenacted the feeding of the hungry stove. "Hello, down there." "Can you find the door?" "Should we keep holding onto your feet?"

By the time dinner was completed and we were preparing for bed, we gave up on keeping the fire alive and climbed into our sleeping bags. The straw and large tarp floor along with sleeping pads and the bags themselves separated us from the snow beneath, keeping us warm – until around four in the morning.

A freezing hurricane-like wind heralded an impending storm, and the snow that was piled on the canvas tent flooring flaps disappeared in a matter of seconds. Now the tent walls seemed to disappear as they were caught up in the wind, and we were completely exposed by the bitter cold outside.

Jack appeared from nowhere, shovel in hand and proceeded to pile the snow back in place. The wind was always one step ahead of him. It was an impossible task, and eventually he signaled the girls to follow him to the van. Some refused to leave the temporary warmth of their sleeping bags, and tried to hop their way along the now, non-existent path. It reminded me of summer sack races with lots of laughter and falling all over one another. Others attempted to ditch their bags, racing barefoot toward the van, not wanting to take the time to get appropriately dressed first. The storm was now directly on us, and what started as a rather upbeat adventure turned into a frightening dash for survival. Now, in addition to the high wind, a rare winter lightening storm appeared to be quickly approaching. The girls scrambled into the van, hoping for safety in our temporary mobile home. One started crying and another suggested we pray.

After prayer, Jack stated that at first light, we drive out of our snowy prison, but to the girl, no one was ready to go home. "Can't we stay here for the day?" "The storm will pass, and we'll be okay!"

So stay we did, huddling together in a cold van not daring to run the engine and the heater for very long, waiting for the storm to pass and the rising sun to provide its light and heat. We sang every song we knew, told new and old jokes and even made up stories. And the storm did pass, leaving a barely distinguishable tent site. We dug in the snow long enough to retrieve a few clothes and shoes with a promise that when we had sufficiently warmed up in the lodge, we would attempt a return to pack up everything else including the tent and sunken and now buried stove.

The lodge was about a quarter mile away. We knew it would take some major digging to uncover the van for travel, so we opted to walk in wet clothes and shoes and try to dry out and warm up. We were knee-deep in fresh powder with each step, and it was exhausting. By the time the giant doors to the lodge were opened for business, we were ready for several hours of warmth and sleep.

The lodge was home to one the largest fireplaces I have ever seen. It covered nearly one twenty-foot wall. Realizing that a number of people might be coming through in our condition, one of the employees had constructed an enormous fire. We loosely huddled in front of it, soaking up its warmth. Someone suggested that hot chocolate was the one missing ingredient, and several of us peeled off to the small café next to the large room that would become our home for as long as it would take to thaw out.

Kay, one of our teens, noticed a television about thirty feet away. The first Superman movie with Christopher Reeves was just beginning, and she left her fireplace position, plopped down on the couch and was immediately transfixed and transformed. Kay needed a real larger than life hero; a kind, humble rescuing hero that could come in and sweep her off her feet – literally.

Kay's life had been filled with tragedy and abuse since her earliest years before her placement into foster care. In spite of nightmarish and unshakeable memories, she had a remarkable sense of humor and zest for life. She loved every activity with our small group. It really didn't matter what we were doing - one of the convincing reasons that quantity time always trumps quality time. It was her moment to escape and hang around positive people.

Now Superman transported her into a new world of strength and tenderness and unconditional protection from everything and everyone, sprinkled with a little humor. Someone pushed a cup of hot chocolate in front of her, and she accepted it without comment. Nothing was going to detract from her private moment with Superman.

The lodge began to fill with those wanting to eat or just warm up or meet friends and family. Soon there were dozens of people, families with small children, ice skaters, cross country skiers, all with their own stories of the storm the night before. A small group of rather tall, heavy-set logger-type men entered the lodge. They were talking football and the play-off games. Spotting the television, one of the men broke from the group and walked quickly to the television. He looked at his watch and stated emphatically, "There's a play-off game on right now." As he reached toward the remote to change channels, Kay, without making eye contact, firmly stated her position. "Touch that dial, and I'll break your face."

He took one look at her and then at his buddies, shrugged his shoulders and slowly backed away. He had met his match and knew this was no time for confrontation. Those of us watching this encounter were laughing so hard we could barely stand upright.

But while there was certainly humor on the surface, there was an underlying sadness. Kay really did need a hero, and nothing was getting in her way of hanging out with one. She had far too few people standing in her corner. So for just a few hours, her larger than life Super Hero took her away from her life in shambles.

When the movie ended, our loggers moved in, changed the channel and the road to the Super Bowl was back on track. We wandered outside in the bright afternoon sunlight to retrieve our battered tent, buried stove and personal belongings, dig out the van and head for home. I knew the movie and weekend had been a short-term fix for Kay. Eventually she would meet and embrace the only real Hero that could and would carry her through life – God's guarantee!

There may be few remarks I question as much as the statement, 'I do not have the time to spend hours with my kids (grandkids, husband, wife – you fill in the blank) but when we are together it is always quality time."

Ask any vulnerable child the question, "Would you rather just hang-out for a day and do whatever comes to mind, or would you like to have my full 100% attention for an hour?" It will always lean in the direction of the full day together. Good conversation or "quality time" rarely happens on demand. We need to be prepared as parents, spouses or friends to be willing intentionally to plan huge blocks of time just to hang out.

When Good Enough Isn't

It was early February, and Tom Everson from Boys and Girls Town came to visit and meet some of our children at a boys' snow trip. He was doing a comprehensive study of vulnerable children, and Today's Youth Matter was chosen as one of the surveyed ministries.

Tom meshed with our boys immediately. He played with them, listened intently and seemed to enjoy every moment of our time together. On Saturday night, after a full day in the snow, he asked if I would like him to do a brief "Bible" study at the church where we were spending the night. I was more than grateful for his help, anxious to see how he (the professional) would convince twenty-five eight to twelve year old boys to sit quietly for a twenty minute God time.

Tom disappeared and returned with a very fake blue plastic dial telephone I suspect he found in one of the pre-school rooms. He sat down and looking at the boys, asked, "Do any of you have questions you would like to ask God?" A quiet took over the room. Then one youngster shot back a question on everyone's mind. "How can we do that?"

Without hesitation, Tom picked up the plastic phone stating, "All you have to do is dial 1-800 and your favorite seven numbers." He methodically began to dial and after a short pause let the boys know the phone was ringing. One by one, the boys edged closer to him.

"Hello. Is that you? (pause) Oh, hi. Is God around?" He looked down at the boys and with one hand over the mouthpiece whispered, "God's on the court playing basketball with Jesus. Moses is going out to get him."

Several boys started to laugh but caught themselves. What if this phone thing was for real? What if Moses was really looking for God on Heaven's basketball court? Surely God would not appreciate hearing rude laughter at a time like this.

There was a long pause, and then Tom began the conversation. "Hello. This is Tom from Boys and Girls Town and Today's Youth Matter. But I guess you know that. God, I have a whole lot of boys here who have some questions. But I guess you know that, too. We've been playing in the snow all day, and I am wondering if it is okay if they ask you some questions?" Another pause. "Okay, God is ready to answer anything you might want to ask Him."

At first the questions came slowly, bordering on the ridiculous. "Is Mickey Mouse in Heaven? "Do I have to wear clothes in Heaven?" There were a few laughs, but Tom answered each question, thoughtfully and with deliberate intent relaying God's message through this blue plastic fake telephone. Within minutes, the questions took a sharp turn.

"What does Heaven look like?" "Will God, I mean you, forgive me even when I've done really bad stuff?" "Ask God what he thinks about drugs." "If I have sex before I get married, well, will God forgive me for that." "Is my Dad in Heaven? Remind God that he was murdered six months ago."

Tom struggled with a perfect answer to a particularly difficult question. The question was just too important. The answer really mattered. He would get a quizzical look on his face and just listen. The boys sat perfectly still and silent, anticipating a significant, life-changing response. I found myself sucked into their questions. What is it like to wonder where your murdered father is? Do the decisions I make now affect me for eternity? Just how far can I push the envelope before God proclaims, "Enough"?

The questions kept coming, and Tom kept answering. After nearly an hour, Tom looked at me for permission to bring the session to an end. Then Tom asked, "Is there another question or two before we close." Every hand shot up. We finally concluded late into the evening when several youngsters, exhausted from a tough day on the slopes, began dozing off.

Tom politely thanked God for taking so much time with us, and God returned to His basketball game. Several boys casually walked to the front of the room to pick up the phone and listen for a dial tone they were pretty sure did not exist. But they had to know.

While I did not take notes, I was feeling pretty confident I could duplicate Tom's teaching with our young girls coming to the next camp. It was such an amazing lesson. I knew they would equally have important questions to ask. After all, how difficult could it be?

You've heard the story before. In Malachi, those Old Testament folks try to shortchange God with sacrifices of lame, sick, blind or near dead sheep. They knew what God had commanded. Only the best would do. Give God the best that you have – always. But perhaps because there was a false sense that nobody was watching, they thought they could slip in the inferior, the less than perfect, and no one would notice. We know the rest of the story. God was not pleased, and once again, He had to reprimand His people.

Perhaps many of us are just as guilty today. Of course, we are no longer under the rule of making sheep sacrifices. Jesus took care of that for us. But I had to wonder if sometimes when I don't think anyone is looking, I slip into that less than perfect, barely get by mode.

God ends up getting what we consciously recognize as not quite good enough.

I have had way too many "not quite good enough" moments. I usually chalked it up to not enough sleep, not enough time or not enough interest. The minute I hear myself muttering, "What was I thinking? Why did I think I could pull this off?" I am in trouble.

Now twenty-six girls were waiting for an exciting evening after our full day in the snow. I gathered pre-teens and four adult volunteers into a small room. I located that same blue plastic phone and carefully hid it under a desk. Boldly and with abundant confidence, I asked if anyone had questions they would like to ask God? Silence! Deadly silence! Tom did not prepare me for a non-response. I didn't know what to say or quite where to take the conversation. So I just continued as if the questions would eventually flow.

Picking up the phone without hesitation, I proclaimed, "You can talk to God by dialing 1-800 and your favorite seven numbers." And I started dialing. And they stared at me as if I truly had just been released from a local mental lock-up facility. There was Moses, the basketball court, and the whole set-up. But not one question. No amount of my humming and hawing over the phone made any difference. Finally, one brave girl asked, "Do we have to stay here, or can we play a game or go to bed or do something fun?"

I nodded with great disappointment at my inability to explain that God really cares for His children and wants us to know His simple message of love. Vulnerable children just trying to survive do not make the best life decisions. Conveying God's heart could have been a life-altering moment. Instead, I did not do my homework. It was a robotic, lifeless, not good enough lesson and it fell short – way short.

There are many people who have since told me, "It could have happened to anyone. It was just one of those things."

I knew better. I didn't take the time to prepare and plan for any and every possible scenario. I knew that just good enough definitely was not good enough.

DONKEYS

In our earliest TYM days, donkeys were a huge part of our teen programs. Their key assignment was to carry the majority of heavier and bulkier supplies on our backpacking trips. It allowed our campers to carry only personal items, thus lightening their own load. Donkeys can carry well over one hundred pounds of stuff, and the campers were more than happy to load them to the max.

I received some very good advice from the wife of one of our leaders as he attempted to explain how to tie a diamond hitch over the pack so everything would stay in place. He was a seasoned packer and used seasoned packer lingo. She signaled me to come over to where she was standing some twenty feet away from our class of newbies. "Marilyn," she whispered. "Protect your ignorance." Words I have been practicing on a variety of topics to this day!

There is an obvious reason for that familiar statement, "You're as stubborn as a donkey (or mule)!" Donkeys in fact have a mind of their own. They have no concept of sharing or cooperating unless there is a tangible reward in it for them. If their role for the week is not clearly defined on day one, sometimes administered by the strongest on staff, it is not uncommon to see bucking and running, kicking and occasionally biting.

It often became a love/hate relationship for teens and donkeys alike.

For most of our girls, it was love at first sight. Maybe it was their long ears, inviting endless conversations well into the night. Maybe it was that braying noise kids always try to duplicate but rarely do with any success. The campers got to lead their assigned donkey for the day and feed and water him. Sometimes girls had a real fear of their beast – one of the reasons for our beauty contest on the girls' trips.

When we announce, "Tomorrow we are having a beauty contest in the morning," each girl could only wonder if she would be picked as the most beautiful on her team. No one dared talk about it, lest others make any stinging remarks. When morning rolled around, we would lead the donkeys into a circle and instruct each team to take one donkey to make beautiful. Of course, we brought along fancy clothes, make-up, fingernail polish and even toothbrushes. We learned early on that without toothbrushes in our arsenal of supplies, one of the girls would sacrifice her own to make sure their model had sparkly whites!

Replenishing our clothing supplies was no easy task. Going into a local Goodwill to ask if they had anything that would fit an eight hundred pounder, only brought stares and sometimes laughter.

There were long discussions and mild arguments about the perfect outfit from our limited selection. Comments flew everywhere. "I don't think that color will match her eyes." "He is a little too big for that number." "Pink or red toenail polish?"

Several donkeys accepted the pampering without protest while others fought it tooth and nail. The girls always won out one way or another. One of the true joys of a donkey beauty contest was all the laughter coming from each team. Hooves were painted into toenails. Mascara and lipstick were administered liberally. At the end of it all, the teams paraded their donkey masterpieces in front of the judges, pointing out all the finer features of design and color coordination. It never seemed to matter who actually won the contest, and we often declared every participant as a clear winner.

I sometimes wondered if the donkeys judged themselves or simply looked at each other in disgust. At least that is what it looked like to me.

Usually on the boys' trips and rarely on girls' trips, we would hand each team ten feet of surgical tubing and assign them to make a really good slingshot. Without knowing the purpose of the task, the base was often good enough to launch something into the stratosphere. Then each member on the team was handed a pair of inexpensive surgical gloves. The instructions were to go out into the meadow and find something to launch. Any rocks would disqualify the entire team.

Inevitably they found that not-too-old/not-too-new "donkey biscuits" were perfect for the task at hand. I am pretty sure some of you may be wrinkling up your face in a dreadful scowl at the thought of even suggesting such a thing. Others may smile and remember a similar game you played as a child with "cow paddies," usually without the benefit of gloves.

If you could have seen the transformation of pretty tough inner-city teenage boys once the contest began, you might reconsider the value of such a ridiculous challenge. With an arsenal of ten "biscuits" in hand each team launched one at a time with measurements taken and marked for height and distance. The team would recalibrate after each attempt. It was reminiscent of the javelin or discus competition at the Olympics. Of course after the contest ended, the boys would discard their gloves, wash their hands repeatedly and dive into a nearby lake.

Those of us born before 1950 probably remember the era of what I like to call "The Age of the Shrink." Everyone was in therapy – sometimes for years. It was the mark of those really wanting to know what was going on in their lives – and might I add, having the financial resources to pay for it. We were all determined to untangle the mess our parents made of us in our formative years. Most of us knew deep down there might have been a better or at least less expensive way to go. By 1980, fortunately that was replaced with a different approach. If you were not better within six months, it was time to find a new shrink.

In the camping world, therapy translated into the importance to deprogram and assess what a child had learned from any given activity. It was the camp equivalent of psychotherapy. I suspected stressing this part of camp came from retired psychologists and therapists. It might have gone even further except that children and their families reminded us that camp in fact is suppose to be fun. While I am sure there is value in going through this deprogramming process, for years I struggled to come up with what to say or even how to suggest an intelligent conversation after beauty contests or donkey biscuit launches. Why did we even make this a part of our backpacking program? Was there any intrinsic value I could measure?

I eventually came to the conclusion that these two very silly activities – a beauty contest and a donkey biscuit launch – can in fact change a child's perspective. First, it was something completely out of their wheelhouse. No one had ever practiced this type of activity, thus it had a tendency to level the playing field. Second, it produced gut-wrenching laughter. There are two things that seem to disappear from any family structure once things begin to completely fall apart – laughter and light. One has only to refer to Norman Cousins' book *The Anatomy of an Illness* to identify the value of laughter. Laughter literally saved his life when the best doctors were unable to identify what actually was wrong with him and therefore find a cure.

Laughter breaks down all sorts of barriers. And ridiculous laughter can smash those barriers into oblivion. I would never suggest that hurting kids have no need for therapy. Sometimes it takes years to untangle all the dysfunction a child has been forced to endure. But a huge part of that healing process may very well begin after youngsters discover the uncontainable joy when they no longer need to hang onto their cool and simply let go and be a kid again.

Raul was definitely cool. His cool started to disintegrate when, in order to catch up to his donkey for the day, he actually had to do a bit of running. When you wear baggy jeans well below your hips, keeping them from dropping to your ankles is no problem moving at snail's pace in the inner city. But when your donkey takes off in the wrong direction and it is your job to bring him back under control, Raul soon discovered the limitations of moving fast enough to catch up while holding onto his pants to keep them from falling. Quietly he asked the backpacking leader to rig up a belt out of some extra supplies. He was clearly an endangered species adapting to a new environment moment.

During those first few days, Raul would often disappear barely out of sight but up to something he did not want us to see. We eliminated some of the more obvious negative possibilities such as smoking or drinking alcohol, because the telltale marijuana or cigarette smoke smell was absent, and he certainly was not behaving as if he were under the influence.

At our final awards ceremony before beginning our walk back to the trailhead, we offered the boys the opportunity to join us on an upcoming whitewater-rafting trip. Raul could not contain his excitement. He was a good swimmer, and I am sure he knew it might turn out to be the trip of his lifetime. Before we started our hike back, he voiced his desire to be a part of that trip – repeatedly.

As we loaded the final gear, I made a short sweep of our camping area. It has always been our policy to leave the landscape in better condition than when we first arrived. Sometimes the donkeys were loaded with a whole lot of trash we gathered left behind by other campers.

About twenty feet up the hill from where Raul's team had set up their campsite, there was a bark-free snag still standing upright but completely lifeless. And it had been tagged with florescent green spray paint. The circular pattern looked familiar. Raul brought on the trip a small art notebook and several pencils, and the cover page matched exactly this same spray can pattern.

Tagging is such an identifying mark in most large cities. To the untrained eye, it may look like the scribbles of a three year old who does not understand why we struggle to see his lion in the jungle. There is an underpass in the middle of the city of Oakland that served for years as tagging central for any and every person wanting to practice their skills. To most, it was a messy eyesore. Then an amazing artist was commissioned to cover the walls with a creative, jaw-dropping mural. The word went out quickly, and it has been left alone for the most part by tagging want-to-be artists.

I pulled Raul from the group until we were standing directly in front of his latest artistic endeavor. I raced for the right words, that while I understood his artwork might have been appropriate in the inner city, it was a completely out of place in the wilderness. There was no talking his way out of this one. He apologized profusely and promised it would never happen again. As we walked back toward the others, I made sure he knew as a result of his unwanted tagging the whitewater rafting trip had been taken off the table for him.

Raul started crying softly at first so no one could hear him, and eventually he broke into out-of-control sobbing. It seemed as if the weight of all of this was more than he could bear, and he grabbed my shoulder and begged, "I can clean it up if you let me."

So while the rest of our campers, donkeys and leaders started the slow trek back to the cars, Raul and I walked quickly back to his campsite. I gave a few suggestions but never lifted a finger to help. This was his moment to persevere and shine or give up and quit. He scrubbed with dirt, water, rocks and his bare hands. Two plus hours later, we left the snag with only a remnant of the original tagging. I was confident that after a winter in the high Sierra, the tree would most likely collapse and disintegrate under the weight of all that snow.

By the time we caught up to the rest of our group, the donkeys were loaded, the gear cleaned and each boys' personal belongings were back with its rightful owner. Raul moved quickly to make his backpack transfer and leave behind memories of those last few hours. I am fairly certain it did not take long for him to discard his makeshift belt and return to the Raul his family and community might recognize.

Raul did participate in the rafting trip, and he pulled me aside to vocally declare his backpacking experience was a life changer for him. He admitted that having to correct his tagging mistake was powerful and that he intended to up the ante on his drawings and move past tagging to something a little more serious and lasting.

Nine years later, a small package arrived at our office. Inside were several near-professional hand-drawn pictures of mountains and donkeys, a marmot and a stump with faded tagging on it. The enclosed note read, "I will never forget."

Nor will I, Raul. Nor will I.

I Am Just Praying for Forgiveness

Jill was tall and slender. She never smiled. At first I wondered if she kept her teeth under wraps because of poor dentistry. That is often the case with many of our children. Thanks to some pretty sacrificial dentists, we were always able to refer children in need free-of-charge. But Jill did not to need to see a dentist.

Her brutal early years had taken its toll. All joy seemed to have been sucked out of her, and she was just going through the motions of a pre-teen at camp. There were a few moments when she started to relax and enjoy what she was doing, but these were always short-lived.

As has been written in previous chapters repeatedly, there is never a magic wand in human hands that can instantly undo years of living amidst dysfunction. It takes trust, and trust takes time. Until a child can begin to trust again, the healing process is at best delayed, at worst, always out of reach. It dogs us well into our adult years.

Jill was not interested in interacting with anyone. While she participated in activities, it was always at a safe distance. Any game or activity in which she felt she might mess up was off limits. It was as if she were under constant paralyzing fear of what might happen next.

At an early morning staff meeting while campers were still asleep, her team leaders – all three of them – expressed concern. "Jill seems so distant all the time." "Sometimes I think she is talking to someone invisible." "I hear her at night muttering to herself as she is falling asleep in her sleeping bag." There was no one person who seemed to have broken through her impervious shell. We left that staff meeting determined we would all keep our eyes open for possible ways to reach out to Jill. Of course, we knew it would not be easy, but it was certainly worth a try.

On the third day of camp, Jill was pacing back and forth in the meadow by herself, much the way we picture expectant fathers outside the delivery room. Her hands were clasped in front of her and she was quietly pleading to whom I did not know. The way she was clasping her hands together, eyes half closed, it looked as if she were in a heavy conversation with the Almighty. Wanting to hear more, I inched toward her.

She never saw me coming. Jill was intent on her petitions to God. "I am just praying for forgiveness. Please forgive me for my sins. I am so sorry. I am begging you to forgive me, God." I could not help but wonder what in the world her "sin" had been to plead her case so fervently.

Suddenly she looked up, and most likely would have bolted except that I was a little too close to pull it off without a bit of awkwardness. "Hey, Jill. Do you want to sit for a while? There is a big tree just a few steps away, and I brought you some water." She nodded, and I passed her the water bottle. Soon we were sitting together at the base of the tree.

Jill clearly did not want to make eye contact, but she did want to unload. "You know my uncle is a preacher. My foster family makes me go to his church, because they think he might be the only real family I have, and they want me to know who he is.

"Every Sunday – and sometimes on Wednesday when we go to Bible study – my uncle would take me in his office after church. He'd close the door and touch me and do other stuff. After it was over, he'd read some scripture, usually about sinning and how I was a really big sinner. Then he would pick up this piece of wood and hit me for the sins I had done."

Jill was exhausted from telling her story, but there was more to come, built up from years of silence. Waiting for her to finish her story was critical. Maybe God was taking away my ability to say anything so I would not share my anger, disgust and outrage at such a creep claiming to be in a position to share God's Word and His plan for our salvation.

"There were other times when he would not touch me. But he would always ask what sinning I had done, and even when I told him, he'd let me know it was a little too late for confession.

Then I would get hit. So now I just confess for everything I do so God will forgive me immediately."

I did not know where even to begin. Clearly God was not in any of this, but it was also clear that my outrage was a totally separate matter. Explaining to a twelve year old that "missing the mark" was never a good reason to hit anyone would not be easy. The physical and sexual abuses were beyond words.

I wish I had been able to say something remarkable that would have put Jill on the right track. It is never that easy. I did try to let her know that straight from Scripture we are reminded that while we all sin, God's love is so great and His forgiveness so far-reaching, she did not need to spend every waking hour pleading her case. If all of us could ever truly understand this love, I believe we would operate quite differently. Love without strings in my opinion is a bit overwhelming.

Jesus came down pretty hard on those feeling superior they had it all together. But with those struggling with debilitating illness or difficult life circumstances, he poured out love and forgiveness in abundance. Making light of sin is something I do not often do. But under the tree that day I shared a number of the stories of God's demonstrated love for the downtrodden.

Jill seemed to get it. Certainly she had years ahead of her to build up trust in pastors. She only knew of one pastor handing out his twisted sense of justice and ensuing punishment. At camp that week, Jill stopped pleading all the time. She was given a first glimpse of a Savior proclaiming to a woman preparing to die at the hands of her accusers, "Then neither do

I condemn you." (NIV John 8:11) That kind of love is overwhelmingly contagious.

(As a side note, her uncle was eventually sentenced to a long prison sentence. As it should have been.)

FORTY FEET OF SHEER HEAVEN

I believe Solomon's proclamation "There is nothing new under the sun" is as true today as it has ever been. (Ecclesiastes 1:9) Of course there are new discoveries everyday, but they seem to be a part of the building blocks set in place from the past.

The plagiarism of ideas is something I readily embrace. Perhaps thirty-five years ago, I listened to a seasoned camp director give his "Ten Best" at a Christian Camping and Conference Association national convention. I walked away with one idea that has become one of the signature activities of our TYM summer camping programs. Repeat campers ask about it. They know and embrace that it is a well-kept secret for kids who have never been to camp before. Keeping that secret is another story, much like the surprise gift from a five-year-old unable to wait for the recipient to actually open the gift before blurting out its contents.

I came back with a simple design and asked one of our TYM friends for help. He cut two ten-foot long, three-inch PVC pipes in half, length-wise. When put end-to-end they made a perfect forty-foot long receptacle for the mother of all ice cream banana splits. We never hold back on the ingredients. Bananas were on the bottom. Then ice cream in any number of flavors. We drizzled chocolate, strawberry and caramel syrup the entire length. It was topped off with abundant whipped cream and a variety of sprinkles and of course maraschino cherries. (If there were any children with peanut allergies, they received with great ceremony their own private masterpiece.)

Presentation of the banana split takes on a number of different scenarios, depending upon the camp director of the week. Timing is everything. Depending upon the weather, there is a pretty small window from when the banana split is put together to when the ice cream is still cold and edible. If the timing is off on a hot day, the whole thing melts into a sticky mess.

We have used a variety of strange animal sightings to get children on the move to our designated banana split site. Once there was a rumor of a parachute dropping the ready-to-eat dessert. That scenario was hard to convince even the most gullible unable to grasp how that might even be possible.

My favorite, once the set up team was in motion, was to gather all the campers together at our campfire circle. I would let them know of my sheer disappointment with those involved in the soccer game on the ball field and leaving such a mess. Repeat campers had to play along with my tirade, and some could have been nominated for an Oscar-winning performance. I got pretty good at convincing the entire group there would be no swimming until we did a complete cleanup. Most were not willing to protest, even if they were not a part of the destruction.

The look on my face might have been a little too scary. Then we would silently march down the hill to where the finishing touches were being completed, pass out plastic spoons and after blessing the dessert, the kids dug in.

Usually they did not mind our trickery. The reward was simply too great. But there is a twist to this gigantic ice cream spectacle. About five minutes into it, kids are getting full, with a little bit of a brain freeze. We watch carefully to make sure everyone has had his/her share, and at a nod from the camp director, a designated leader begins a food fight!

Then ice cream flies. We set up an "ice cream fight safe zone" for the few kids (and adults) not wanting to participate. Over the years few actually choose this safe area. As expected, team leaders participate with enthusiasm. It is a time for silliness and letting loose and having ridiculous fun.

One eight year old came up to me to ask, "Are you going to let us do this?" Ice cream covered eighty percent of her body, and a maraschino cherry was stuck in a glob of chocolate on her face. Then she noticed I was not much better off than she was. She smiled broadly, shrugged her shoulders and proclaimed, "I guess so."

Sometimes when I visit a church, someone will hear this story and ask, "Don't you hate to waste food like that?" I have to wonder if the food is really wasted or if it is doing its job of breaking down huge walls and giving a child yet another opportunity to be just that – a child.

The cleanup begins with a hose and ends with an all-camp swim. If you were to survey campers, most would say it is indeed one of the highlights of their week. It might be because they had never experienced anything like that before. It might be because we went all out to make it unforgettable. I suspect it is a highlight because it screams, "Someone must really like me!" Yes, we do indeed.

And Now, the Rest of the Story

Being wrong is never fun. But jumping-to-the-wrong-conclusion wrong – that's downright embarrassing and humbling.

On a California December Saturday afternoon, our TYM Milpitas office was filled to capacity with TYM children, their siblings and families and a whole bunch of volunteers for our annual Christmas Party. Our children look forward to this party for months. I'm sure our at-the-time failing economy caused families to scramble to find ways to celebrate the holiday season. A local church came with their high school group to help with arts and crafts projects, from kaleidoscopes to tree decorations, and a wide variety of really fun games.

Two volunteer families helped with every aspect of the party. They had driven eight children to the office and already beginning relationships were budding. But one fifteen year old was particularly struggling. Several years prior, he was present when his father was shot on the street. His anger bubbles over, and without a significant man in his life, he has no clue how to deal with it. He is frantic to find a mentor but does not know how to ask for help. His scream for help often is translated into angry outburst and an attempt to control anyone younger or smaller than he is.

Ten minutes into the party, our fifteen year old began to get restless dragging along a number of other boys with him. There was that split second to decide a new direction before the situation would move from slightly disruptive into complete and utter disintegration. Without a word, one of the dads disappeared outside with the group for a never-ending game of football in the parking lot. They would come inside to refuel and then return to their game. How wonderful it is to watch a father show interest in young boys who have no positive male role models in their lives.

Toward the end of our three-hour party, the church high school group performed an amazing skit without words of God's love for us and of His desire to pull us out of the things that drag us down. The best part of their drama was that all our children "got it." God is doing His best to separate us from destructive circumstances.

There were no disagreements of any sort, and our TYM children and their families were genuinely appreciative. It certainly was a successful party by anyone's standards. Even Martha Stewart would have deemed it so.

One of our TYM families arrived late. Three of their children were already at the party, but their mother, her sister, step-dad and grandfather, along with six other children immediately jumped into activities. Mom was first introduced to TYM through her children. I clearly remember a Christmas party years before when we sat down together to share about the miracle of Jesus, and she confessed she had more questions than we could cover in a few minutes. We have since met a number of times to go over some basics, and a little over a year ago, she became a completely sold-out Christian. She struggles to raise five children on her part-time job and a welfare check, but her faith is solid. Trusting Jesus is something she does quite well.

When it was time for the party to end, mom was nowhere in sight, and someone told me she had taken one of our graduated TYM campers (now a sophomore in college) to the Great Mall in Milpitas. Since I was driving three children to a city about an hour away, I waited as long as possible for her return and then locked up the office, leaving her extended family waiting in the parking lot for her return.

I am pretty ashamed of where my thoughts took me. Why did she leave to go shopping, undoubtedly for herself or her children, in the middle of the party? She must have received her pay or welfare check and was going a little selfishly crazy. Doesn't she know how inconvenient she has made things for me and for her family?

And now, the rest of the story...

When I dropped her three daughters off at their church the following Sunday, their mother apologized for returning to the office after we had all gone home. She told me that she had taken the responsibility of getting our young college student home. In her own words,

"I was watching the skit those wonderful young people were doing, and I happened to notice one child sitting on his knees. The bottoms of both his shoes were exposed, and there was a gaping hole in one of them. The other shoe seemed to have separated and the sole was pulling away from the shoe. God spoke to me that I needed to go and buy him a pair of shoes. I brought the young man along with me because I knew he knew Milpitas and could get me to the Great Mall.

"When I returned and you had all left, I managed to get hold of your program person for the address of this child. I drove to his house and gave his mom the shoes. She was crying with gratitude, and we got to pray together. It was definitely God prompting me." Once again, I found myself speechless.

Following Jesus causes people to do strange things. Some travel far away from home to live in a strange land and share the Good News, all because they felt a prompting from God. Some find their way into a homeless encampment with a load of blankets because they heard a storm was coming. Still others charge into a burning building or dive into murky waters because they were needed in that moment. And one young woman with five children of her own to feed and clothe and drive to school saw a need and decided to follow Christ away from food and festivities and buy a pair of shoes for someone in need.

It is a great example for all of us.

Memories

It is funny the way childhood memories have a real stickiness to them. Like it or not, they cling onto you throughout your life no matter how hard you try to brush them aside.

Before I could walk, my father made sure his three daughters were completely submerged in classical music. He would play record after record from Mozart through Beethoven and onto Chopin and make us guess composer, style and title. (I guess you have to be a certain age to remember records.) We went to every Saturday children's symphony in San Francisco. White gloves. Hat. Dress. We loved and hated it. But no matter how we felt at the time, it became part of the definition of who we were. We were the three girls marching off to yet another concert. Classical music nerds.

Not much of a surprise that of my dad's fourteen grandchildren, twelve play a musical instrument well enough to join a high school band or orchestra. Family reunions are filled with songs and laughter and music of every sort and style.

Memories – good and bad – have a way of molding us into way too familiar shapes. Athletic families seem to breed athletes. A four year old in any computer geek family can program my now-extinct VCR or DVD player, de-bug my computer while surfing the Internet for the latest data on the nesting habits of the Ruby-throated hummingbird. Expected. Michael Phelps's kids, will surely have webbed feet!

Bad memories likewise have a way of sticking to us. The abused becomes the abuser. The drug addict raises drug users. Grow up in with smoking parents and your chances of smoking skyrocket.

Young girls will admit that while they hated their dads for all the horrible things he did to their moms or to them, they find themselves attracted to men with those same attributes.

We persist in dragging our past wherever we go. It becomes a very heavy suitcase stuffed with all those memories chained to our wrist or ankle, and we can go nowhere without it. No matter how heavy and cumbersome the baggage, it is extremely difficult – nearly impossible – to let it go. We fill it with the past we cannot shake. We may choose to trust or not to trust, to tell the truth or lie our way through life. Our past becomes a part of us and seems to define us, at least in our own eyes.

While teaching school one year, I asked each student to build a simple balance scale out of two small paper cups and several tongue depressors. They were not made to last, but they certainly illustrated the power and weight of our past on our present. The two cups hung precariously from string attached to a tongue depressor crossbeam. Several made scales worthy of weighing even the most miniscule amount of any substance known to man. One boy suggested that his balance could be sold to an old west movie set for display in the assay office. Others were held together with paste, glue and, most likely, a wad of chewing gum.

I gave each student a package of m and m's with the instruction that after the exercise, they could eat what was in their cups or left over. Now they were anxious to get going – as quickly as possible.

"Here are your instructions. By the cup on your left write on a piece of paper, 'This is not true for me' and by the cup on your right, 'This is true for me.' I am going to read a number of statements. Place one m & m in the cup on the right when it is true for you or one m & m in the cup on the left when it is not true for you."

I gave them a few moments to open their bags of m & m's and write the instructed words next to each cup. Now we were ready to begin.

"Remember, listen to the statement, and then pick the cup on your right if the statement is true for you. Put one m & m in that cup. If it is not true for you, put an m & m in your cup on the left."

They all nodded as if to say, "Enough with the instructions. We get it already."

"Most people tell me I am smart." M & m's dropped into their appropriate cups.

"My dad always calls me his little girl (or man)." More m & m's.

"I am a really good student."

"My parents often read to my brothers (sisters) and me."

"I just can't seem to do anything right."

"My family usually eats dinner around a table together with no television."

"I fight a lot with my parents."

"I'm a pretty good athlete."

"Sometimes I hear my parents fighting."

I read through a list of statements. Most were obviously positive. A few were pretty negative. Still others were fairly neutral, an individual judgment call – neither blatantly positive nor obviously negative. Before I had reached midpoint, most scales were tipping in one direction. Several students had broad smiles as they realized their positive cup was now nearly overflowing. They were ready with the high-fives and "way to go" when they corporately noticed that one girl in the back of the classroom seemed to be overwhelmed with sadness. She was struggling to keep back her tears. Although she certainly was not a part of the preppy or jock groups, everyone liked her and seemed deeply disturbed by her sadness.

Then they noticed her scale. One cup sat firmly on the table. The other was swinging slightly with the weight of only one or two candies. It was clear she had little in her life that was to her liking.

Much later I realized this was one of those defining moments for our classroom. It was a Coach Boone moment in <u>Remember the Titans</u> when the team put aside their differences and came together. One by one, my brilliant class decided to take matters into their own hands. Without a word, they stood up, walked back to her desk and one-by-one started dropping their own m & m's into her nearly empty cup.

Within moments, the cup began to descend slowly to the desk raising the other cup in the process. The shear weight of their gifts lifted the cup and her spirits.

But there was no stopping. The m & m's kept piling up into a mountainous cone until they spilled over onto her desk and eventually onto the floor. That was the signal for the games to begin.

The whole class erupted into uncontrollable laughter as m & m's were eaten and thrown around the classroom. Our school custodian must have wondered what was going on that day. No one was thinking about the school custodian. It was a moment for the ages. Every child learned a lesson way beyond anything I had planned. Initially, the goal was to recognize just how life's events can tenaciously cling to us long after they are over. It had been preempted by a spontaneous unashamed display of unconditional love and caring.

It wasn't until the next day that the class wanted to talk about what had happened.

"That scale/cup thing was way cool." "Can we do it again, only this time *we'll* come up with the questions?" "I never realized how much I love the fact that my family eats meals together – even during my favorite television show." "Yesterday I learned that the comments I make without even thinking really affect others. Good and bad." "We did okay with the whole thing, didn't we?" "It's important that we take care of each other."

It was hard to find the words to describe just how proud I was of all of them. I guess I didn't need the words because they were really proud of themselves. The lesson was clear. Although dragging around our heaviest burdens is what we do best, it doesn't have to be like that. We have earthly friends to help balance the load. And although I could not say it in a public school setting, we have a God as an eternal friend who is more than capable to empty any bucket anytime and take it on himself. What a friend.

Years later, Emma taught the same lesson with a twist.

I met her in the camp parking lot. She was reluctant to get out of the vehicle that transported her, and I suspect that if offered, she would have been delighted to return immediately to the place where she was living. Emma looked as if it had been a very long time since she had laughed or even smiled. It wasn't a sad look. It was more of that drained, emotionless look that screamed, "Leave me alone. I just want to be left alone. No questions. I've answered enough questions to last a lifetime."

Thirty-three little girls received an exuberant welcome those first few minutes. They were greeted by twenty-three team leaders and staff lined up with shouts and a "We are glad you are here" song. The games began before we left the parking lot. Soon campers and leaders knew names, ages, hometowns and favorite scars.

All except for Emma. She wasn't playing. She had discovered a caterpillar next to one of the vans and was fascinated watching it crawl up her sleeve. This little creature was not about to pry into her affairs or try to pull her into another senseless conversation. Emma was just a few weeks with her new foster family – the fifth of the year. She was not ready to let more strangers creep into her life. The suggestion that she join in the group game was soundly rejected, and immediately a volunteer slid next to her to admire her small companion. There was no conversation needed. This was a time of adjustment, and it was going to happen at Emma's pace. Together they watched the caterpillar crawl up her sleeve until it appeared it might disappear down her shirt collar. With a half-giggle, Emma was ready to change course and engage in the already midway game of "Birdie on a Perch." It is a fast-paced partner game that takes little skill and seems to produce smiles and laughter in abundance. (Call any youth pastor or camp director for game details!)

The next few days were a blur. One thing was clear. Emma trusted our Camp Director and was ready to follow her anywhere. The director's activity – from preparing lunch for distribution to a casual walk to the swimming area – became Emma's activity. They were rarely apart for long.

Emma eventually warmed up to her team leaders. Their willingness to demonstrate love and acceptance without strings or questions worked its magic. While memories of abuse are still fresh, it becomes almost impossible to lay them aside, even at camp. That old heavy suitcase is pretty persistent. It is extremely difficult to want to share anything with anyone when new foster parents are constantly prodding, pushing and peddling their endless questions.

Every night at campfire, the director shared a thought or story about God's love and concern for each and every one of us. Yet, recognizing that when neglect is still fresh and raw with campers, she decided to share a personal conversation with God. She started the drama by ripping out pages in her "journal" throwing them on the ground and telling God how tough things are.

"God, people sometimes make fun of me because I am overweight. Where are you when that happens? Why do I struggle with so many things?"

The girls sat ever so still as the director's conversation with God covered a wide range of feelings and emotions. It was pretty obvious that the campers were relating to what she was saying. She was hitting close to home in areas they knew all too well. Most knew it was just acting.

Not Emma. When she could stand it no longer, she got to her feet, approached the director and whispered, "It's okay. Everything will be all right." Then she wrapped her arms around her waist and just held on patting her gently on the back.

It was a precious moment for all of us. A young girl simply could not stand to see an adult hurting the way she herself was hurting without offering comfort. If only we could all learn Emma's lesson of love!

It is Better to Have Friends

Carrying the weight of years of abuse and neglect is daunting. With some children it seems just a little heavier than for most. Harry was one of those kids.

He was confused at the whole idea of a primitive camp and teams and our tipi village. It was all so new and unexpected. He was one of the last to join up with a group, and probably would have taken a pass on this whole team idea except that the camp director steered him toward the team with the fewest campers. He looked awkward and out of place. I might have expected him to spend endless hours playing video games on a living room couch with a bag of chips, cookies and a soda within arm's reach. There was a clear lack of coordination.

Harry smiled all the time and at everything. He laughed at even the not-so-funny jokes – the jokes only the teller understood. It was his method of choice at attempting to secure a friendship. He loved to cook and even more to eat. Since each team was responsible for its own meals, everyone loved Harry around mealtime. He cooked with considerable skill and even made suggestions to raid the kitchen for some cheese, onions and tomatoes for the omelets. Harry raised one eyebrow when asked, "What's an omelet?" Cooking over an open fire did not slow him one bit. It was a bigger challenge, but one he knew he could master with ease.

Not so with any physical activities. Harry watched longingly at the other swimmers. It did not matter that most could not swim and wore life jackets. He feared the anticipated ridicule the minute he took off his sweatshirt. It took three days and extremely hot weather for Harry finally to shed his sweatshirt and get into the water – one toe at a time until several adults surrounded him and repeatedly assured him he would not drown. Not on their watch.

He avoided the high ropes course. Just too dangerous. And any field games. Too much speed required and therefore off limits. But our small basketball court was another matter. Harry looked longingly at the other boys on the camp's half-court. He hung back just far enough to never be quite part of the game, yet close enough to feel the action.

One morning, his team leader suggested that after breakfast and before the first group activity the two of them could grab a basketball and play a little one-on-one. Harry could not get to the court fast enough. He dribbled the ball awkwardly without making any attempt at shooting toward the basket.

Perhaps it was the distant thud of a ball repeatedly hitting the ground or just a group of boys having the same idea as Harry, but before long five or six youngsters were gathered on the court waiting for any pick-up game.

One ten-year-old commanded, "Shoot the ball, Harry." Without thinking, the ball left Harry's hands in the general direction of the backboard.

The man responsible for most of the camp's development made the decision to build our own backboard. It ended up a monstrous mother of all backboards. It was huge. Perhaps eight times bigger than regulations demanded. It was hard to miss.

But Harry missed. Badly. His team leader grabbed the ball before it bounced off the court. He handed it back to Harry and firmly commanded, "Try it again." Within moments, everyone was part of Team Harry, determined to stay with him until a basket was made. "That was close." "You'll make it next time." "One more time, Harry." Harry took a shot. Another camper chased down the miss. A word of encouragement. Another miss.

Harry kept shooting and missing. His entire entourage kept retrieving the ball and putting it back into his hands. After more attempts than anyone cared to count, the ball rattled through, and his fans exploded. There were words of praise and congratulations. He was slapped on the back and carried off the court. Harry was Michael Jordan, Steph Curry and Shaq rolled up into one small, round boy.

That one simple basket changed everything for Harry. He was first choice on everyone's team. No one seemed to care that Harry was not all that athletic. He demonstrated mankind's longing to overcome huge obstacles and harness success. Each boy at camp that week saw his own enormous failures, only instead of denying or running from them, Harry was forced to confront and conquer. How wonderful it would be to have that many people in your corner when things went south.

At the final campfire, Harry wanted to talk about his amazing week. Mostly he just wanted us to know things would be different in his life. After thanking absolutely everyone – team members, team leaders, support staff, all the animals and redwood trees – he concluded, "I learned this week that is better to have friends than to be alone."

Camp had become his community, his church and family. How blessed to be a part of such as this.

The Picnic Basket

My introduction to the not-for-profit world came through work as a Volunteer in Service to America (VISTA). It was a two-year commitment that blew my eyes wide open. I drove to Seattle for my initial VISTA training with around twenty others. We were all college graduates, some with masters' degrees and one with his doctorate. For some reason, it seemed logical to give up two years of what others might have deemed a time to get a "real job" in order to make a difference and change the United States of America in the process.

Our official training began with the entire group participating in a poker chip game. We were given instructions to come to the front desk and pick up thirty red, white and blue poker chips. That was it. No instructions as to their value, how many of each color or what we were supposed to do with them. We were obedient to the letter. No questions asked.

The next step – again without detailed instructions – was to randomly begin to trade the chips. Most of us were drawn to one color or another. A few decided to keep an even distribution of colors. After we completed ten minutes of our trade game, we were told to sit down. It was at that point our facilitator told us that each chip color had a specific value. That immediately placed all of us into two distinct groups – the very wealthy (a pretty small group of "haves") and the rest of us - mostly extremely poor or on-the-edge poor/middle class. All based on the rather random choices we had made.

Within seconds, the wealthy took over, as wealthy people have a tendency to do, and began making and changing the rules to their advantage. After all, they owned the most, paid most of the taxes and immediately elected themselves to power. Every time the poor or even the few in the poor/middle class thought we might trade chips to level the playing field, the rules would change. In a final act of desperation, we pooled the few chips we had of value and gave them all to one of our own. The plan was that after becoming a part of the wealthy, he would help change the rules to benefit our majority.

The turncoat left us and never looked back. It was at that moment our entire poor class turned over chairs and tables, linked arms and began singing "We Shall Overcome" while staging our first sit-in. Before things turned ugly, our instructor stepped in calling an end to the game. He spoke softly, "Now you are ready to serve the poor. You know why our poor feel so helpless." Yes, we did.

Four days later, our close-knit group felt prepared and ready to change the world. With shouts of encouragement and hugs all around, we headed to our separate sites, vowing to keep in touch. We never did. Our paths took us in many different directions all over the western United States, but we were forever bonded in the knowledge that there were others ready to tackle the world right alongside us.

Living on the edge, working with the disenfranchised and trying to make a difference can become a nightmare. We anticipated making a difference quickly with our brilliance and dedication, but the glaring reality was that there is never enough money and never enough workers to do everything needed to make the impact we expected. When successes come, there is a tendency to hang around that success a little too long. It is equally difficult to walk away from inevitable failures.

Several years into the non-profit world and shortly after my VISTA years ended, I was working on yet another fundraising effort to try to sustain a program guaranteed to alter the direction of our community.

We had invited a traveling circus to town, and a portion of each ticket was earmarked to end up with our non-profit. Someone had the brilliant idea that if I paraded around a local shopping mall in a Yogi the Bear costume, people would race to buy tickets to the circus and fund us for the next million years. At that point, I was willing to do almost anything.

Dressing as an exact Yogi Bear look-alike brought unexpected results. First, the costume provided little ventilation and the temperature inside soared until it was almost unbearable – no pun intended! Because you are looking for direction through Yogi's mouth, the poor internal circulation became instantly stagnant. Every few minutes, I slipped into unoccupied walkways to toss Yogi's head and gulp down quarts of water.

The costume did draw attention, and we did in fact sell tickets. Definitely not enough to fund the program for very long, but after several hours, we deemed my Yogi experience a success, and I got ready to make my escape exit. At that moment, a young lady, perhaps twelve or thirteen years old, came running up to me and threw her arms around me. "Yogi! I can't believe it is you. You are my best friend in the whole world." Now she backed off enough to size up all of me. "Yes, it *is* you."

As she backed up, I caught enough of a glimpse to size her up as well. She was clearly a Downs Syndrome child. And she was clearly delighted to be near me. She would alternately hug me and then put me at arms' length to make sure it really was the Yogi she revisited every Saturday morning. Suddenly, she got a quizzical look on her face and backed away from me.

Wagging her finger in my face, she began her stern lecture. "Yogi, stop stealing picnic baskets. It's just not right." She repeated that mantra for about three minutes, and all I could do was boldly shake my head to confirm that I would indeed become a reformed Yogi.

With a final reminder, she hugged me and skipped off into the mall. Yogi had in a few minutes affirmed what she knew to be true. Yogi *was* real and because of her would turn from his thieving ways and begin a new course toward outstanding citizenship. She was a happy camper.

A few minutes later a young father and his little boy walked toward me. The dad exclaimed with excitement, "Look, Timmy.

It's Yogi Bear – just like in the cartoons." Timmy took one look at me, and even through my obstructed vision, I could see he was terrified. His piercing screams rattled windows, but as I started to retreat, his father interrupted. "Timmy, it isn't real. It's just a person dressed up like Yogi." He turned toward me and pleaded, "Would you take off your head and show Timmy that you are not real?"

The head came off, and although Timmy was not sure if I would turn into a scary, picnic basket stealing monster in an instant, the screaming turned into a quiet whimper. At his father's prompting, Timmy reached a tentative finger toward my shoulder but could not muster the courage to actually make contact.

I said a few forgettable words, put my Yogi head back on, and began a last sweep of the mall.

And then it hit me. Whose reality did I want to claim as my own? Did I want to play it safe and clearly know the difference between a make-believe cartoon character and a real-life loveable bear willing to give up his thieving ways because someone cared enough to tell – and demand – an attitude adjustment? Was I most comfortable with a young girl's knowing that her very own, very personal Yogi was standing directly in front of her? Or was it more adult to put away my childish ways and remove my oversized Yogi head to discover the more acceptable human me?

That moment changed my perspective of Downs' children. Her reality was not all that bad. In fact, I think I rather prefer her world of imagination, and yes, Yogi and his picnic basket!

Your Own Personal Rooting Section

Serving others is complicated and more often than not a little messy. That may be one reason why so many of us drag our feet in an attempt to avoid becoming too involved. We become obsessively involved with family or church or our vice of choice – watching too much television, playing a sport or fanatically following our favorite team, going to way too many Bible studies – and in the process we pass up an opportunity to do the very thing Jesus continually reminds us to do. Love and serve others. That was Christ's message.

I remember speaking at a small church, and I felt particularly compelled to make sure they understood the importance of service. It was an impassioned speech, and I thought my brilliance was compelling. Several came up to me afterwards to show interest in becoming involved in our work with vulnerable children. No one followed through. One woman apparently interested in what I was saying, nodded frequently during the talk. Afterwards I approached her and asked, "I noticed you seemed interested in serving others. What are you passionate about? Where are you serving right now or where would you like to serve in the near future?"

Without a moment's hesitation, she responded, "I am serving my two dogs." Then she went on to provide the details about their grooming, walking and eating routine and how much time it took out of her every day to make sure they lived the good life.

She certainly was passionate about those two dogs, and while I am certain there may be dog lovers everywhere lining up in her corner, I had to wonder if that is what Jesus had in mind when he said to Peter, "Feed my sheep."

Perhaps the whole idea of service was never better demonstrated than when the high school group from First Chinese Baptist Church of San Francisco volunteered to sponsor a girls' snow weekend. They came well prepared.

They raised the money to cover all expenses, including transportation, the food and arts and crafts supplies. They purchased disks and inner tubes for sledding. They also recruited forty-two high school students and ten adult supervisors to oversee everything – for our fifteen TYM girls! Talk about overkill! I worried in advance if our kids would feel overwhelmed or completely swallowed up with all those teen high school students. And I wondered if bringing along some of their high school guys would create a problem of a different sort.

We spent Friday night at a church about a thirty-minute drive to deep snow and great inner tube runs. Within minutes of our arrival, the extent of the high school team's willingness to serve was put to the test. One of our TYM girls was pretty carsick, and she was tenderly led into the bathroom by three teen girls who stuck with her in her sickness and were ready to do whatever it took to make her feel better. The rest of our TYM girls were organized into small groups for an arts and crafts project. While the teen boys prepared dinner, friendship bracelets and some pretty amazing origami were created. The games continued well into the night. They even included a few games with Chinese words our youngsters learned quickly. Every TYM girl was soaking up all that lavish attention. They had no idea what was in store the following morning.

After breakfast, we loaded up for a short drive to some pretty deep snow in an isolated spot. Inner tubes and plastic disks were dragged to the top of the hill. There were long inner tube trains of teens and kids, single riders, snow ball fights, an enormous igloo (researched for architectural design and engineered by a teen Frank Lloyd Wright clone) and endless hot chocolate (whipped cream and marshmallows included) for everyone.

The girls could not have asked for more. Their mantra was heard over and over. "Look at me." It was shouted before every activity – from making snow angels to yet another inner tube run. And absolutely every time it was uttered, at least six pair of eyes fixed on that TYM child. It continued from the time we hit the slopes into the late afternoon when we declared the weekend a success and headed for home.

Somewhere along the way, I stopped for a bathroom break and ask the girls how they thought the weekend went. I particularly wanted to know if they felt overwhelmed by too many volunteers from the church. After several girls spoke lovingly about the church group and all the fun and when we might get together with them again, the spokesperson for the group summed it up the best. "It was an amazing weekend. They were all so wonderful. It was like having my very own rooting section."

I have always fantasized about running through the tunnel of the 49er stadium (I do after all live in the San Francisco Bay Area) with some of our TYM kids (along with perhaps Jerry Rice or Joe Montana just for good measure) with the sound of seventy thousand screaming fans ringing in our ears. That would have been an amazing rooting section. After our snow weekend, I realized it really doesn't take that many people cheering us on. It only takes one or two people believing in the value of a vulnerable child, giving that child reason to believe in a God of compassion and a God of all comfort.

Cold Cereal

One had to wonder the brilliance of bringing twelve teenage girls from the inner city to spend a week on their first backpacking in the high Sierra. No electricity. No cell phones. No bathrooms. No I-pods or MP3 players. Just necessities you can carry on your corporate backs for up to seven miles of hiking each day.

Some teens jump into it with enthusiasm. It is new and adventurous, and the incredible beauty of the high country minimizes the downside of having to carry a share of the load. Sometimes there are unexpected patches of snow. Nothing quite compares to a surprise snowball fight on a warm afternoon in the middle of July in your shorts. The clear sky can turn in a matter of minutes to torrential rain and a heart-pounding lightening storm. Spotting a golden eagle, a shy marmot, a field of purple and yellow lupine or a snake on the trail can be a thrill of a lifetime even for teen girls.

Today's Youth Matter (TYM) offers caseworkers, group homes and homeless shelters an opportunity for some of their teens to attend a five-day backpacking trip at no cost. We have no idea the history or background of the girls they refer. There are dozens of possibilities, but it is usually less important to try to find root causes for behavior problems than to just begin to form relationships that may last for years after the trip is over.

Courtney showed up for the drive to the trailhead with most of the symptoms of an abused teen, but at the same time she displayed confidence and a firm leadership style that impressed all the adults on the trip. She carried more than her share of the food and supplies necessary for the week. Her enthusiasm for the wonders that surrounded her spread like wildfire with her peers. They seemed to feed off her energy, and she set a tone for the five days leaders long to see.

The trip leader, Tucker Farrar, is a master in the wilderness. Not only does he have a deep love of children – particularly vulnerable teens – but also he is keenly trained for every possible difficulty the group might encounter on the trip. Tucker has an endearing way of going through backpacks before the trip even begins to cut out unnecessary weight. Out go deodorant, shampoo bottles – even soap. Of course, all electronic devices are confiscated along with extra shirts, extra pants and even extra underwear. At the time of this ritual, the teens complain bitterly. By the second or third day of the trip, words cannot describe their gratitude.

The first day's hike was uneventful. Only a few miles. Not too steep. There were few rest stops, and the entire group divided into three smaller groups for the hiking, cooking, eating and sleeping. All appeared normal and without incident until the first breakfast when Courtney declared that she did not eat cereal. Her team leader relayed that message on to Tucker.

Tucker knew there was a specific allocation of food and that it was important to stick to the menu. Start eating food intended for lunch first thing in the morning, and there would be nothing left for the last few days. Tucker also knew to make sure Courtney remained hydrated and that with hunger, she might change her mind. She did not complain but ate nothing, and they packed up for the day's hike.

The incident was forgotten until the next morning when once again, Courtney would not touch her cereal. Again, the team leader found Tucker and told him that she felt there was more to her story than just not liking cereal. She promised to do a little probing.

Tucker dug into some of his emergency food supply and made sure that Courtney ate a granola bar and drank her quota of water. Still she refused to complain about skipping breakfast.

Sharing horrible memories is never easy, even amongst healthy adults. We rarely open up to friends, even acquaintances and share our less than stellar moments. It takes time to trust. And for vulnerable children, trusting is often the major issue. It is something that simply cannot be rushed.

So the leaders waited and continued to be available. That may be the single most important thing we can do with vulnerable children. Simply be available. After the hiking, after dinner and after most had gone to bed, Courtney pulled her team leader aside from the rest of the group.

"You know, I was taken away from my parents when I was little. And I've been in more foster homes than I can count." There was a long pause as she swallowed hard to keep from crying. "The home before the one I am in now – I was there for a little over a year. I tried to tell my caseworker about how bad things were, but she never listened. She didn't want to believe me, because that meant she would have more work to do. Finally, after a year, she finally listened to what I had been telling her all along, and I got to move."

Again, she paused and then continued, "For one year, the only food they ever gave me to eat was cold cereal. I had cold cereal for breakfast, lunch and dinner. Except when I went to school. Then sometimes I got to eat the cafeteria food."

It was hard to hear. How could a child pleading with her caseworker about the food she was forced to eat go unheard for so long? Were there no home visits? No check-ups?

There is a reason for that old cliché, "Hindsight has 20/20 vision." No one would fault anyone of the adults on that trip for standing firm that most likely Courtney was a picky eater used to getting her own way. Just another spoiled teen that was completely unappreciative of the free trip offered to her.

Everything changed on the trip with that simple piece of information. Meals were turned upside down to accommodate Courtney. And probably of greater importance, she had a new trustworthy family willing to bend and do what was right. That counts for everything.

CYNTHIA

Moving often and living with a family of five in a car had taken its toll. Questions begged for answers. What does it feel like to live in a temporary shelter with a single mother, a brother and three sisters?

How do you cope as a stunningly beautiful fourteen-year-old when you cannot walk outside your one bedroom apartment in the homeless shelter for fear of assault or abuse happening in the hallway right outside your door? And what is it like to realize that while two younger sisters are United States citizens, your mother, brother and you may be deported at any moment? And the burning question of what God has to say about homelessness. What do I do about that?

Cynthia was fourteen and somehow slipped into a camp for eight to twelve year old girls on the guise that she needed to oversee her two younger sisters. She was out of place; obviously expecting camp to be different than it was turning out to be. Maybe it was the fact there were no boys, no electricity, no flush toilets and no comforts of the good life she had seen on television and wanted for herself.

Somewhere in the first hour of camp, Cynthia decided she would withdraw from all activities, look out for her sisters and endure until she could escape on Saturday. She also decided she simply would not smile. Every leader took their turn talking to Cynthia. They tried punishments and rewards; bribery and pleading. Nothing was working.

Mid-week, the talk of camp was the challenge of our high ropes course. "It's really scary. But it is so much fun." "I've never been so afraid in all my life. I couldn't stop my knees from shaking." Cynthia decided to take the five-minute walk with her team to face our six high ropes elements – all twenty-five feet off the ground.

There are some extremely valuable lessons on the course. You need a good harness, some very strong rope, some complicated knots, carabineers and a whole lot of trust in the person on the other end of the rope. There are a series of what looks like very large staples hammered into the tree that make possible the climb to the element you intend to cross. Before the climbing begins, the person responsible for making your climb completely without incident checks your equipment – helmet, rope and harness. Then the instructor states, "On belay" and waits for the climber to respond, "Belay on" after everything is rechecked for safety. The word "belay" roughly translates, "I will be there for you." Or "I've got your back." It is important information for children to understand who truly has them on belay 24/7, and it cannot be more clearly demonstrated than on a ropes' course. Then, just before beginning the climb up the tree a new request is given of "Ready to climb" and the response, "Climbing."

There are two wonderful parallels to our everyday walk in the world. Almost any real sense of accomplishment comes with effort, and deciding to trust someone you may not know very well with your life is never easy. If the person on the ground is not paying attention, the climber can be in real trouble. There is a certain tension of the rope – not too tight and definitely not too loose. Ropes courses can be wonderful learning tools when done correctly.

Before Cynthia had stepped into her harness, her youngest sister was already beginning her climb. She made it look so easy. She danced up the staples effortlessly. She ran across the log, ringing the bell and was back on the ground in a matter of minutes. Cynthia muttered, "That looks easy."

Sarah, her team leader, helped her into the harness and showed Cynthia how to tighten the webbing around her waist and legs. Then she stated with confidence, "I am going to have you on belay. Will you trust me?"

Cynthia nodded hesitantly, and they walked to where the exercise was to begin.

Sarah checked her own harness, all carabineers, the rope and their helmets. After all the commands were given and everything was rechecked, Cynthia slowly pulled herself up until her foot rested on the first staple step, then onto the next and two more after that. She was about six feet off the ground, when visibly shaking, Cynthia stated, "That's far enough!" But Sarah knew better.

Our ropes course policy is always "challenge by choice." The climbers can decide just how far they want their challenge to take them. It might be just a few staples up the tree. The challenge might be to complete every element on the course.

"Cynthia, I know you are a little nervous, but I know you can do this. I will not let you give up so easily." Before Cynthia could repeat her demand to come down, Sarah added, "I can stay here all day, but I am not letting you come down until you at least try to climb the rest of the staples." Period.

Our ropes course supervisor – always on the course when there are climbers to make sure everything runs smoothly and without incident – started toward Sarah to remind her of the "challenge by choice" policy. There were no words exchanged, but the looks between supervisor and Sarah said it all.

"This is important for Cynthia. Do not overrule my decision to encourage her."

So there she stood, clinging to the tree and narrow staples with the sense that if she were to fall she would surely die. The tears began to flow, and the standoff began. Cynthia clinging to the tree refusing to go any higher. Sarah holding the rope tight, refusing to back down. Then, without notice, Cynthia began her slow ascent until she rested on the log attached to the tree that was her particular challenge element to cross.

Ever so slowly, she began inching across the log. Those on the ground could see her legs shaking and recognized this might have been her toughest challenge, perhaps equal to dealing with homelessness. Then the bell on the other side started ringing, and Cynthia broke into a broad smile and screamed, "I made it. I actually made it!"

In a matter of seconds, she was on the ground hugging Sarah, the ropes course supervisor and anyone within reach. Everything changed in a matter of minutes. She had gone from loser – afraid to do anything outside her comfort zone – to a one-of-a-kind winner!

Sarah smiled broadly and whispered to Cynthia, "I knew you could do it! If you can do this, you can do anything!" Cynthia knew exactly what she was talking about. It might just include her hated math class she was already planning to fail or even the school musical.

Cynthia's lesson is one that belongs to all of us. Get out of your comfortable, safe zone and you might just experience an unforeseen miracle right before your very own eyes.

A Home of our Own

During TYM's first six summers, we rented camp facilities within reasonable driving distance. Sharing the camp with other groups proved to be problematic. We could never predict the ensuing blow up between our TYM kids and the other campers and non-TYM leaders in attendance at the same facility with their own programming. After all, they had never taken a Camp Behavior 1-A class and had no idea that "borrowing" items from the camp store without paying for them was actually a bad idea.

We eventually moved to smaller camps where we could take over the entire facility and lock up the camp store for the week, but nothing was a good fit. We wanted our kids to experience cooking their meals over an open fire and living for a week without electricity – all at an affordable price. One camp had the perfect lake but the facility was in complete disrepair. (When a youngster walked out of one of the bathrooms with a door handle in his hand, I knew we were in trouble!) Another camp had the world's greatest water slide, but way too much poison oak. Still another had a really great stream, but the drive was prohibitively long.

One of our Board members finally stepped up to suggest that we look for a perfect piece of bare land and harvest some of the timber on it to pay for the property. The entire board committed to pray and seek God's wisdom in our search. I learned quickly just how desperate some realtors were to sell their less-than-perfect sites.

One site passed through a garbage dump; another through a pigsty. An excited realtor called to inform me that she had found the perfect "virgin timber" site with a small lake and easy access. The four hour drive was capped off with another one hour drive up a windy dirt road – guaranteed to cause queasy stomachs all around – with a small "lake" about five feet wide by ten feet long and about six inches deep. Did I mention it was on a windswept hill and that most of the timber had recently been removed?

It turned into a two-year search fraught with disappointments and futility. Needless to say, we were discouraged. We questioned God's will that we find a permanent camp home.

Then, quite unexpectedly, we met Bud McCrary, one of the owners of Big Creek Lumber Company. Within thirty minutes of introductions, Bud was driving into a forty-eight hundred acre parcel located in the northern Santa Cruz Mountains – an hour and a half drive from almost anywhere in the San Francisco Bay Area! He drove to what was obviously his favorite spot. Tall towering coastal redwoods, bluish purple irises and a carpet of delicate forget-me-not flowers.

Bud stated rather matter-of-factly, "If I were building a camp, this is where I would put it, but you are welcome to look over the entire property to find something that you like." And look we did, but Bud knew what he was talking about. The property was perfect.

The next few weeks were a whirlwind as we prepared for our first summer. There were improvements to be made – tipi sites, outhouses, an expanded ball field and one lone building that would serve as our storage room and food distribution center. It would take an additional year to add the pond and pool and three buildings for storage.

The county where the camp was located had a number of regulations for us to meet. Since we were operating less than eight weeks of the year (summer season only), we were able to file as a campground instead of a camp. Regulations were not as stringent as with camps. Still they wanted plans and drawings for the property, an evacuation plan and a way to insure food would be properly stored. In fact, the local czar of the California Unified Retail Food Establishment Law (CURFEL, as we affectionately called it) insisted that we have a completely established kitchen available. Trying to explain that the kids would be doing the cooking in small groups did absolutely no good. He was emphatic. Without a CURFEL kitchen there would be no camp. At one point, he pounded his fist on the table and stated, "As long as I am here, you will not operate." Within a few days, he was forced to take a six-week leave of absence for health reasons. I had to wonder if God was working overtime for His kids! (We did find a CURFEL kitchen for food storage at a nearby church.)

The final hurdle was a request to submit some architectural plans of our one building, the stage at the campfire circle, and an outhouse to the building department. Once approved, they would pass it on the planning department for final approval. I remember spending the better part of a day with a board member and large drawing paper, fine pens and a good ruler. I am not a very good architect, but thanks to my eighth grade art teacher, I can block print with the best. Not wanting to wear out our welcome, we visited several restaurants with large tables and good coffee until we were satisfied with our work.

As we were standing in line waiting our turn at the front desk, a very distraught woman explained that her contractor had hung one of the doors in her beach house with the hinges on the wrong side, and the building department was forcing her to go through the entire permit process all over again. Our board member and I looked at each other and gulped. We were certainly dead in the water!

With our necessary copies, I remember forcing a smile and laying the clearly hand-drawn plans on the counter. "Will these work?" I stated with confidence. The man behind the counter looked at me as if to say, "You've got to be kidding! Are you out of your mind?" but only said, "No!" Then he typed something on the computer, got a quizzical look on his face and disappeared into the back room. A few minutes later, he reappeared shaking his head and handed us the plans. "Take this over to the planning counter."

The planner looked at our architectural drawings quizzically. Then he typed something into *his* computer and disappeared into the back room. He was shaking his head as he stamped "APPROVAL" on our designs. Back to the building department for their final approval, and we were out the door overcome with gratitude at what we were privileged to watch. I have no doubt that the God who could speak the universe into existence had no problem understanding the intricacies of local county computers!

Bud and Big Creek Lumber helped build our fishing/boating pond and swimming area. On more than a few occasions, the company provided the muscle to repair the roads after a particularly wet winter. Big Creek is definitely old school – helping neighbors, donating their heavy equipment in any emergency and caring deeply for the environment and children. Bud and his brother, Lud, know that treating others with respect and dignity is the only thing to do. Their code of ethics is above reproach. A handshake is as good as a written contract. Lending a helping hand to neighbors whenever needed is the right thing – the only thing – to do.

They have the reputation as "the loggers even environmentalists have grown to love and respect."

One summer, Bud was standing by our pond watching little girls dancing in the water. The laughter was uncontrollable. Some were learning how to swim. Four girls were spinning as fast as they could on and in a large inner tube. A large group of campers were involved in a beginning synchronized swimming class with three swimming instructors. Bud smiled. "I guess we *can* grow kids and trees on the same property!"

After sixteen years at this site, San Mateo County rules became a bit more stringent, and sadly we were not able to keep the site. The search continued for that elusive "camp of our own."

SCIENCE CAMP

I think many Christians have a deep fear when the word "science" is spoken. Perhaps it brings back memories of the Scopes monkey trials. Don't scientists bombard us with evidence that we evolved from apes? Don't all scientists believe in evolution? Scientist and God seem to appear in direct contradiction of each other.

After all, doesn't the big bang theory appear far more "scientific" and logical than a God who spoke the universe into existence? Perhaps my favorite explanation to unanswered scientific questions comes from a group of Jesus followers who proclaim, "God did it! Now, let's find out how!" By 2016, scientists agreed the Big Bang happened in less than a hundredth of a billionth of a trillionth of a trillionth of a second! Sounds like God to me!

So in the summer of 2009, TYM conducted our first science camp for some budding kid scientists, curious about much around them and under-exposed to hands-on experiments in the classroom. We hired at near minimum wage a gifted middle school science teacher who prides himself in challenging children to never settle for taking the easy way. (After camp concluded, he donated his wages back to the ministry!) I watched him teach in ways I enviously wished were mine in prior years when I worked in the school system.

We hand-selected young people showing interest at camp in discovering snakes, lizards and stars and had a giant dose of endless curiosity. Matt (their teacher for the week) had them from the first simple experiment of water displacement. They magically made a small water bubble rise to the top of a capped bottle. Some kids thought it was magic. Others probed for a more scientific answer.

Matt had an endearing way of getting each camper's undivided attention. He gave instructions just one time. He was always ready to help if the project didn't go as expected. But when a child was not paying attention or was distracted at the time the directions were given, Matt would calmly respond to a question about the project in a quite voice and simply respond, "Do whatever I said." They learned quickly to listen in the first place.

Then they moved on to paper rockets. At first they were in total disbelief that paper under pressure could actually soar to a hundred plus feet. One budding astronaut spent hours redesigning his masterpiece for maximum lift and even took time to project where it would eventually land. He was tired of turning into his own search and rescue party after every launch. Most campers looked with envy as his rocket soared to new heights but did not have the patience or know-how to redesign their own.

One day they were challenged to build a shelter meant to protect them from the elements. They were given sparse supplies. Three large garbage sacks, scissors, string and duct tape. After dividing into groups of two or three, they were sent into different directions. No stealing ideas from another team. Some looked great from the outside, although I suspected would not last in a real rainstorm. Others paid attention to details – the kitchen, living room, bedroom and even an almost complete bathroom – toilet paper included! After about an hour, Matt toured their structures asking vital questions about structure strength and workmanship. He gave all teams the opportunity to rebuild and strengthen their foundation, walls and roof.

Great teachers have an amazing instinct to recognize the attention span of children age ten to twelve and to give them just the right amount of time to complete this building project. Some were content to try to duct tape their garbage sacks to a circle of trees. Others reinforced everything with wooden walls built out of sticks and logs of all sizes and shapes. They were able to build a wooden roof and only use the garbage bags as reinforcement.

Their final instructions were to settle into their shelters and wait for the storm. When the storm arrived, gratis a very small sturdy fire hose, it did not take long for each group to grade their own design. Several collapsed in a matter of seconds amidst squeals of what it might really be like to live in such a makeshift house. The teams that had taken the time to build a foundation and actual walls withstood the deluge. Their pride (and perhaps a little too much overt bragging) lasted throughout the entire week. They kept returning to their shelter just in case a real storm was coming their way.

There were several good lessons from the shelter assignment – from the Three Little Pigs to the scripture about building a house on the Rock instead of upon sand. Planning and preparation usually pay off.

The shelter lesson led into an assignment of building an unsinkable boat to cross the pond. While the entire team was instructed to build the boat, only one member was required to actually paddle – or sail – to the finish line. Our campers were allowed to use any non-edible items in camp. The teams were mixed up to allow for new partnerships to form. Kids are no dummies. By now, most realized that jumping on the team with at least one bright mind was a pretty good idea and much better then sticking with their best camp friends. There were deep discussions about possible materials. Life jackets, empty five gallon water jugs, dry logs, rope of all sizes and of course several rolls of duct tape were among the most popular items chosen.

Perhaps the most valuable scientific lesson in the boat-building project was that of learning to embrace failure and make adjustments. Empty five-gallon water jugs are not very stable. Filling each bottle with some water usually brought a bit of stability. The lightest person in the group was not always the right choice as paddler. Having paddling skills was equally as important. Matt stood at a distance watching each team. He said

Science Camp

few words or gave any suggestions. It was their project to fail, fail again, learn from their failures and finally succeed. Brilliant!

It was sheer joy to watch the faces of each team as they launched their boat, shouting paddling instructions incessantly, cheering successes and already planning boat modifications for the second round. One boat sank within seconds of leaving the dock. The team had not calculated the effects on boat stability with the weight of the one occupant. That information caused the untried boat builders to scramble and make immediate adjustments. As expected, the joy of success and the learning curve of failure were great lessons for not only our week together but for life moving forward.

There was a wildlife component, stargazing and bug and lizard collecting. Every camper walked away with a new appreciation of the world of science and its effect on their academic world. They kept a journal during the week of things they had learned and of the importance to always ask questions, challenge theories and draw conclusions for themselves. Six years later, one of the participants from that camp called me to let me know he had been accepted at Pomona College in the fall. He wants to be a structural engineer. He thanked me for nudging him in the direction to reach a little higher and try a little harder. I doubt that anyone could have stopped this young man. His IQ soared into the stratosphere and although he attended a low-performing high school, there were many teachers who saw his potential and encouraged him as well. How wonderful to be part of the village!

GIVING AND GIVING AND GIVING

Street-smart boys have a hard time understanding why a large group of teens from a local church would actually want to come and play at the park or in the snow over a long weekend with them. They love it; they just don't quite get it.

Kim, the youth pastor from a local church is one special lady. Kim takes seriously the importance of teaching her teens the unique value of and commitment to service. In fact, to even qualify to join their serving team on a building project or a Daily Vacation Bible camp in a Central American country, each member of the team must complete several local service projects. They always come ready to work hard and lay it all on the line.

There is never a lack of activities or one-on-one time with our children in anything they do with them. They seem to be able to go all out, non-stop for the entire time of service. One year, forty-two teens and five adults came to prepare camp for our opening in a few weeks. There was no job beneath them. They cleaned and then painted outhouses and two storage buildings, mowed high grass on our over-sized play field, cleared trails, pulled tall weeds from the pond – the list was very long, and there was never any complaining about tired muscles or our very long day.

We had included several TYM campers hoping they would get a few important lessons about putting in a hard days' work and working alongside others. I asked one fifteen-year-old what he had learned specifically from his day walking alongside a very skilled contractor. Without hesitation, he emphatically replied, "Measure twice. Cut once." Sound advice for all of us!

It did not take long for the church group to quickly embrace our TYM kids. The lines between them blurred almost instantaneously, and they became a single-focused group.

As we were preparing to depart, we gathered together for prayer for the summer, grace for all the campers and a brief message about the Master Servant. Following Jesus means signing up for long hours, sore bodies and deep joy. One of the teens shared the story of Paul, beaten and chained in prison, singing praise songs for all to hear. Joy is always possible in all circumstances.

Following that short reminder, the entire group wanted to sing. For nearly a half hour, requests kept flying and a very talented guitar player kept us on key and on track. Standing in the midst of towering redwoods, praising God for His guidance and love and creation seemed only natural. Many raised their hands to the heavens. Others held hands to corporately make sure God saw their unity. To all the doubters in the United States of America who loudly proclaim that young people are not like they used to be, I wanted to shout back, "You are right. They are not like we used to be. They are so much better!"

As the singing began to wind down, one final request came from a three year old, "How about E-I-E-I-O?" The entire group needed no prompting. Old MacDonald would have been proud.

Seven Pair of Underwear

Most of us have decided that growing up we all experience a degree of verbal and emotional abuse. Primarily in my life it came from "the look." Some of my friends have no idea what I am talking about when I mention "the look." They seem to be the exception. Most of us can recall more than a few occasions where "the look" prevailed. Perhaps many of you had an all-knowing dad when it came to dispensing the look. Dads somehow administer the look – at least in my family – better than moms do. It can cut to your core and scream, "I am not happy with you right now." There is not much a child could do to instantly repair the damage that brought forth that look. That might take time. It should be mentioned, the look most often is administered in a calm, non-threatening manner. While it hurt and felt terrible, I never thought I had to run for my life or fight back. While vowing I would never use "the look" with my own children (although I suspect I have unknowingly done so), its crippling effect was never long lasting. Either my father forgot my transgression or it lost some of its steam over time.

Unfortunately actual abuse comes in all sorts of sizes, shapes and degrees. Physical and sexual abuse goes way beyond the look. They leave long term, defining scars well into adulthood.

But the variables of the types of abuse paint only part of the picture. The children and their reaction to what is going on says a lot, and it must be studied carefully before long-lasting help might be available. Abuse that begins even before a child is born wrecks havoc on that child for most likely a lifetime. Born addicted to a variety of drugs that mama used while pregnant guarantees a life of pain and never-ending adjustment. It does not necessarily mean a life is 100% wasted. It does mean excruciating pain from withdrawals as a newborn and a propensity for drug use later in life.

Mary was born addicted to drugs. She was beautiful and shy, confused and way behind in school. She knew way too much about sexual abuse from multiple sources. Before her biological mother died, she was clean of all drugs for several years, but she could never quite get over her own guilt and remorse for Mary's struggles. Mary somehow tried to blame herself for her mother's death. "If I had been a better daughter…" "I should have tried harder.…"

With no immediate available relatives, Mary entered the foster care system at age ten and after more than a dozen poor placements, she was moved to a small group home. Generally, group homes do not try to operate as a family. Point systems are often the rule. You do this or that and you earn points, and with points come privileges. You mess up and points are taken away, along with privileges. That can be good for some children. They know what to expect and how to make the system work for them. For Mary it was a disaster. She longed for family but with her mother no longer alive, her memories of visiting her biological father in prison faded quickly.

Mary was thirteen on our first outdoor backpacking experience together. She really wanted to find acceptance and an authentic sense of belonging. Mary reached out to everyone to the point of bordering on the uncomfortable. Her one phrase repeated throughout our trip was, "Am I doing okay?" There was definitely an underlying purpose to the question, and it was clear only time would reveal the answer.

That answer came more quickly than anyone expected. Late one evening as most were in sleeping bags and ready to end the day, Mary came over to me to ask, "Am I doing okay? Can we talk?" Her story spilled out over the next two hours. It was interrupted repeatedly with uncontrollable sobs. I could do nothing to relieve all the suffering she had endured since her earliest years. We simply held onto each other while Mary's story was poured out at my feet.

Although her mother's drug addiction set the stage from her earliest memories, it was the men in her life that inflicted the deepest wounds. I am fairly certain if Mary's life were mine, I would never be able to truly show forgiveness for their actions no matter what the circumstances. Forgiveness perhaps heals the forgiver more than the one that is being forgiven. It has less to do with the one who ought to be begging for forgiveness but doesn't even recognize it is needed.

At one point before her mother's death, when they were still a fractured family, Mary was dragged out of the house for some reason she could no longer remember. One of her mother's boyfriends made her watch as he tortured and eventually killed her kitten. I watched Mary as she retold that nightmare as if the telling might make things different. Memories like that rarely fade easily. It was well passed two a.m. when Mary fell asleep, her sleeping bag now right next to mine. I remember tossing and turning and begging God to give me the words that might provide comfort. Nothing came in those early hours, but as so often seems to happen, what some call coincidence, at our morning staff meeting we read:

Praise be to the God and Father of our Lord Jesus Christ, the father of compassion and the God of all comfort, who comforts us in all our troubles, so that we can comfort those in any trouble with the comfort we ourselves have received from God.

(2 Corinthians 1:3-4; NIV)

Mary joined one of our teen girls' follow-up groups and participated with great enthusiasm. She was always the first to respond when the invitation went out for a weekend together. On one occasion a local foundation granted us two thousand dollars to bring our small group on a back-to-school shopping trip. We went to a local mall, divided the girls into groups of two or three with the stern instructions, "We will meet back right here every hour. When you find something you would like to buy, ask the salesperson to put it on hold for the next two hours, and then we will go back to pay for it." And finally the words they had heard from me so often, "Don't embarrass me." They all knew exactly what I was talking about. There would be no loud talking, goofing around or shoplifting on this trip!

We met several times before everyone in our group was ready to hit all the stores to pay for their selected treasures. Surprisingly there were no selections that even the most conservative among us would deem inappropriate. When we hit Mary's store, the salesperson pulled me aside to let me know how well Mary had behaved. "I tried to get her to look at all sorts of shirts and pants. She would not try anything on until I reserved her most prized possession." The saleswoman pulled from behind the counter a package of underwear. Seven in the package and each one with one of the days of the week embroidered on it.

Later Mary explained, "Right now I have only two pair. Now I can keep track of where I am in the week and wash everything on Saturday!"

It would truly be amazing if our world could organize in a manner such as this with its joy over the simplest of things. Then we might begin to understand how to handle the bigger things.

I'VE GOT HIM

Plucking young children from their familiar surroundings and dropping them into a completely primitive camping environment can be good – and also problematic. It can be very good as a way to level the playing field. Street-wise boys and often girls usually know how to navigate through their communities. They have a good sense of when to flex their muscles so to speak and when to fade into the background.

Sometimes they step into camp with that shoulder shrug that basically declares, "I'm in charge. Give me space." That usually lasts until early evening on day one. The noises of camp at night are so different from their more familiar city sounds. Campers cling to anyone with a good flashlight with a certainty that if they don't, they are placing their very lives on the line.

I love to take children on a no-flashlight walk at night, particularly if there is some but not too much moonlight. Inevitably, they discover they can see quite well once they allow their eyes to adjust to the darkness. It usually takes a number of attempts before the group is convinced that every time someone turns on a flashlight, we start the eye adjustment period all over again.

Primitive camp can also be sometimes difficult, bordering on downright awful. When a camper feels threatened no matter what the reason – hooting owls, flying bugs, raccoons – striking out into protective mode seems only natural. There is a reason we refer to it as the 'fight or flight' mode. Both have equally ugly consequences at camp. It is hard to place blame on a youngster's actions when they are completely uncertain if they will make it through another day.

Jared stepped out of the bus in the 'fight' mode for his first experience at any camp. He was more than just angry. He was bordering on uncontrollable rage, but for good reason. It would take several days to unravel a small glimpse into his life at home. Losing both a mother to murder and a father to imprisonment within a few short hours should make anyone angry.

His first act at camp was to pick up a handful of decent size rocks and begin throwing them with accuracy and purpose at other campers and leaders. He was immediately separated from the group and told emphatically that rock throwing is only permitted in the lake when others are not present. Jared certainly understood our position. He had heard it before. Randomly striking out rarely works to anyone's benefit. Processing that information was another matter. Stuck in a nine-year-old body with all that rage narrowed his options.

Ten minutes later, he was physically carried back to the camp director for the same set of very clear instructions. Rock throwing at others would not be tolerated. It must not continue. The consequences of not listening would send him home.

The rock throwing continued and staff corporately agreed that camp was simply not the place for Jared, at least not until he was able to control his out-of-control anger.

While the conversation with Jared dragged on, Tom sat quietly in the corner listening and watching. He was a high school student wanting nothing more than to come to camp and serve children growing up so differently from himself. He attended a privileged private school, but like so many of his peers, he had been raised to embrace the value of giving back and loving the not-so-easy-to-love.

TYM leadership seemed to be headed toward figuring out a transportation plan back home for Jared. It was no easy task. Sending children home for disciplinary reasons is always a last resort. Caregivers can react in so many different ways from complete empathy to outright anger and punishment. But the safety of all campers always takes precedence over any one individual child. The risk of allowing him to stay might very well jeopardize the entire ministry. It appeared this would be the very best option.

Then Tom spoke up, "Can we talk outside?" He locked eyes with the camp director. As they moved out of earshot, Tom poured out a new plan. What would happen if Tom shadowed Jared, just the two of them? What if Jared was permanently separated from his team and spent the week exclusively with Tom? After laying out the plan, Tom declared, "I've got him!"

And so that plan conjured up in the head of a young adult mind took all of us off into a new direction.

Tom did not do much talking. He quietly went up to Jared and softly proclaimed, "You and I are going to hang out for a while." It was more of a factual statement than asking permission. They went together and got Jared's unpacked camp clothes and set up shop in an over-sized staff tent. They were isolated to a degree but close enough for the cavalry to arrive should trouble erupt.

The next few days were a flurry of activities for Jared. They were always on the move, and Jared was always deciding the next activity. It had to be a new wild experience for him. The willingness of an adult to move on your terms and at your speed became a recipe for success. When someone queried, "Where are you going?" the answer took on a number of different directions. "We are off to the far end of the lake to throw rocks" or "We're taking a long bike ride on the main road" or "We're going to shoot some hoops." Tom made special arrangements for Jared's swimming lessons with the lifeguard after the other campers left the pool area.

By the fourth day, Jared was softening. You could see it in his eyes and in the way he stood. No longer were his fists clenched in fight mode all the time. For those of us who tend to want to talk kids in or out of behavior with our words, Tom became our teacher for the week. I never heard him complain. He never raised his voice. In fact, he barely spoke at all. I had to wonder if he was aware of what the rest of us saw first hand in him. Simply walking alongside someone hurting beyond measure pays enormous dividends.

In three short days, Jared learned basic swimming strokes, how to find that perfect flat round stone that would skip at least six times, how to shift into a lower and higher bicycle gear and most definitely how to wear a bike or mountain board helmet without complaint.

Jared joined his team for the final campfire and participated in his team skit. Tom was always within arms-length cheering for the team and for Jared. It looked as if Jared might crawl into Tom's lap during the short devotional. That was a bit too much to expect after such a short intervention.

Although later Jared left our area to live with his grandmother, I can only guess the impact that one week had on his life. He had come face-to-face with the compelling hands and feet of Christ delivered through his new older brother.

HORSE CAMP

The phone call came at 6:30 a.m. A small shaky voice queried, "I know I am supposed to go to horse camp today, but do I have to?" I knew Thomas was reluctant to sign up for the camp but felt some pressure from family and friends, and so he caved. Now, in those early hours, the thought of a huge horse undoubtedly with one objective woke him in the early hours. He was certain he would be trampled, and at best, break a few bones. It was only a matter of time.

"Thomas, I would love to have you join us. You don't have to ride. You can come for the games and the overnight in the barn. And don't forget about all the other farm animals you will see." Words of assurance, or so I thought. Thomas wasn't buying. "Okay, if I come, I absolutely, positively do not have to get close to a horse. Right?"

A few hours later I picked him up for the forty-five minute drive to the ranch, along with seven other boys his age. The drive was uneventful, and Barbara, owner of the ranch, greeted us warmly with cold lemonade and homemade cookies.

There were a few things we learned that first hour on the ranch. Sometimes you have to get your hands a little dirty, not everything turns out the way you thought it would, and Barbara knew absolutely everything about horses and kids. She was no nonsense around the horses. That street-smart group of youngsters never challenged what she said or how she said it. They knew better.

The ranch was a magical place. Horses were everywhere – in the barn and in the field. In the corral, they were already saddled. After the welcome and all those cookies, most were ready to experience their first horse, up close and personal. Each youngster seemed drawn to one horse or another. As expected, Thomas held back, and Barbara made note. He followed her with the rest to the corral and listened to all those expected safety rules. Let the horse know where you are at all times. No loud noises. Do not walk behind the back end unless you are expecting to get kicked. Barbara did a quick calculation of each horse and the weight of each child. This was not rocket science for anyone. No broken bones meant no messing around.

Each boy did a quick calculation as well. Eight of us and eight saddled and bridled horses meant that each would have their own mount for the day. Before they had a chance to pick the horse of their dreams, Barbara spoke up. "I am giving you a few minutes to decide which horse you want to ride. You can pick any one of them, except the one on the end. He is very special, and reserved for just one of you. Climb to the top rail of the fence in front of your horse. I will walk around with instructions on how to adjust your helmet and how to put your foot in the stirrup. Do not do anything unless I am next to you."

Thomas took one step closer to the fence and froze. It was easy to read what he was thinking. Safe on this side of the fence. Not so much if I take another step. Suddenly Barbara was next to him with a carrot in her hand. She extended it toward Thomas, and he slowly reached out to accept it without protest. "Follow me, Thomas."

Undoubtedly Thomas wondered how she already knew his name. They walked together in silence until they reached the special horse on the end. Barbara instructed, "Thomas, I want you to stay right here until I get back. The horse's name is Lucky, and you can feed him the carrot through the fence if you like." And she turned on her heels to get the rest of the boys matched with their horses.

There were a number of instructions only horse people know, and Barbara called to three ranch hands waiting in the wings to assist every step of the way. The boys were all riding, dreaming of galloping off to herd cattle or catch rustlers but were reluctantly willing to remain obedient to just walk until further instructions were given.

Now Barbara was standing next to Thomas. The whole carrot was still clenched in his tightened fist, and he was visibly nervous. Barbara spoke in a soft voice, "Thomas, I want to tell you a little about Lucky. I think he was a little like you a few short years ago. He seemed to be scared of a lot of things. He is a rescue horse and was badly treated before we got him. Lucky pretty much stays in the corral, and he knows it really well. He will never be a trail riding horse because he is 100% blind."

Thomas looked up at her in surprise, "Blind? Is he really blind?"

Barbara continued, "You have to let him know where you are at all times. And you have to treat him with kindness. Do you think you could do that?"

Thomas moved closer, trying to see any telltale signs that Lucky indeed could not see him. Slowly he reached through the fence, and began his first conversation with his new horse. "I brought you something, Lucky. It is right here in front of you." Lucky turned his head sideways so that it would fit through the wooden fence and gently took the carrot from Thomas's extended hand.

Barbara again turned away to focus on the other boys, leaving Thomas and Lucky to get acquainted. Without thinking through what he was doing, Thomas climbed to the top rail of the fence and inched his way down to rest just a few feet from Lucky. This surely was not the first time Lucky had encountered a petrified rider. He knew just what to do. Before Thomas had time to come to his senses, Lucky was now within touching distance compelling his newfound friend to reach out and make contact. Thomas could not resist. He reached out to stroke Lucky's neck and try to untangle some of his mane. Thomas questioned, "Doesn't anyone ever brush you?" Barbara, now standing within arms length, handed him a brush, and without a word once again turned away.

Perhaps ten minutes passed before she returned to admire Thomas's handiwork. She smiled broadly as if to say, "Lucky has never looked so good!" Instead she tightened the cinch and signaled she was ready to give Thomas a boost into the saddle. Not one word was spoken. Thomas was on top of the horse he knew a few hours earlier would surely cause him bodily harm and now was riding his steed boldly around the large arena with all the other riders.

By the end of the day, all the boys had learned to trot and gallop. Thomas shared his thoughts around the campfire before we settled into the barn for the night.

"Some of you probably did not know this, but Lucky, the horse I was riding, is blind. At first, I thought we were going to crash into the fence, but he knew just when to turn and he listens really well. When we first got to the ranch, I was pretty scared. Actually I really did not want to even come. I am so glad I did. I will never ever forget today."

Dr. Howard Dean Trulear has poured many years studying and hanging out with youngsters in trouble. He is a professor from Howard University School of Divinity and once told a group of participants in one of his many workshops, "Kids don't need a whole lot. They are happy to sit with me and watch grass grow if they know I will be there. They just want to know you'll stick with them."

A miracle horse whisperer and a blind Lucky were all that was needed for Jared that day.

Tony

Since 2010, TYM has been involved in an annual Walk-a-thon to raise support for our summer camping season. It is a wonderful time for summer volunteers and campers to come together for an afternoon of games, a short walk and a whole lot of food.

Tony was one of those youngsters. He arrived with his sister, his aunt and her seven children. His aunt had called me at the last minute to see if it was all right to bring him even though he was too young to go to camp. Tony was immediately on overload with dozens of games to choose before the organized walk began. As he darted from hula-hoops to basketballs to Frisbees and to a quick snack, he must have felt he had been given Willy Wonka's Golden Ticket. He had recently been exposed to death and drugs, and processing all of the choices now in front of him was more than his seven-year-old mind could handle.

I signaled to one of the summer volunteers to hang out with him. John knew immediately what to do, and grabbed a kid-size football, came near Tony and threw the ball in a perfect spiral. It sailed into Tony's hands, and the games were on. Even during the three-mile walk, the game continued. When they proudly jogged across the finish line together, the football was under Tony's arm and they were friends for life. I am not sure ten words were spoken. They didn't need words to cement their connection.

They sat together during lunch. Until dessert. Tony got up to stand in front of giant cookie sheets of things he had only seen on television. Of course there were cookies and a large cake. Expected. But a local gourmet baker had donated finger-sized desserts – pecan, lemon, raspberry, apple, chocolate – all calling to Tony, "Pick me. Pick me." The decision was overwhelming. Until John, standing directly behind Tony, reached over and carefully put one of each on his plate. Tony looked at him, smiled broadly, and together they walked over to a patch a grass, plopped down and began the experiment of discovering the best of the best.

Before that magical day ended, John pleaded Tony's case to come to camp, even if he fell short of the age cut-off date by a few months. "I'll make sure he is on my team. I'll watch him like a hawk."

So Tony came to camp that first summer and for the following four summers after that. He participated enthusiastically in every activity, although when John was at camp, he opted for whatever John wanted to do. If you were to ask, Tony would tell you his favorite activity was mountain boarding. He was a walking advertisement that perseverance eventually pays off.

As a seven year old, the pads and helmet were clearly several sizes too big for him. Often he sat on the board as he rode down the gentlest slope he could find. Mountain boards can be deceiving. They look just like skateboards only with bigger wheels. But flat ground is not an option. The rider must maneuver down a hill, and there is never a goal of pushing yourself ahead with your free foot. Much like snowboarding, your feet are loosely strapped in with the ultimate goal of speed and remaining on your feet.

By year two, Tony was standing most of the time. Still on the "bunny hill," but he was nicely growing into his helmet and protective pads. By year three, he no longer sat on his board and graduated to the medium slope. He would show up at the course first thing in the morning and would have stayed until sunset, except when the instructors sent him away to experience other activities they thought he might enjoy. One way or another, Tony found his way back to the course.

Year four was another matter. Now he had grown into larger equipment. Now he was no longer interested in the easiest or medium slope. The giant slope with its big jump part way down the course captured 100% of his interest. He had surpassed his need for instruction. It would only take practice, perseverance and a whole lot of chutzpah.

His team leaders rarely had to look for Tony. They knew where to find him. While several other mountain boarders tried to gingerly maneuver this "black diamond" course and always exited their boards before they actually got to the jump, Tony hit it with everything he had. And he fell repeatedly. The instructors on the course never tried to talk him out of it. They did readjust his pads and helmet after each run.

On the next to last day of camp, Tony grew quite a crowd. Team Tony now had a crew to wipe down the board, check the tire pressure and continue to speak words of encouragement. "I am going to make the jump today," he declared confidently. Come to think of it, those were his words everyday.

On his fifth attempt of the day, he sailed over the jump and landed perfectly, coming to a stop at the bottom of the run. It was as if we had all watched Evel Knievel soaring over the Grand Canyon or Tony Hawke doing one of his impossible tricks.

"Next year, I'm coming back as an instructor," Tony proclaimed. Chutzpah indeed!

Tony handed all of us the road map toward success. When the world says, "Quit," our response ought to be, "Never!" Dreaming big against huge odds hands us huge rewards. And for Jesus going up against the biggest and might I add impossible opposition, quitting was never a viable option. We mattered too much for Him to walk away.

The Anatomy of a Volunteer

After more than forty years in the non-profit world, I have come to several conclusions about volunteers.

- Non-profits, schools, and government programs would grind to a halt without them.
- Volunteers come in a huge variety pack. Some are well into their nineties; others come with a family before they reach the age of five. They come from a diverse background of countries and languages of origin. Some are leaning on the extremely liberal side; others are ultra-conservative. They are all races and all religions. Some come with post-doctorate degrees. Others never graduated from high school.
- They all want to change our world, mostly at the local level.
- Volunteers have a deep compassion for the poor and downtrodden.
- They are difference makers, and they are teachable.

- Often they leave us in disbelief wondering why we never thought of the great ideas that come out of their corporate heads.
- It is extremely difficult to box them into neat resumes of volunteer qualities.
- Most – but not all – volunteers may quit or fail if they are not trained and appreciated.
- A few become volunteers because of strong feelings of guilt from living with too much stuff. The guilt quickly turns into compassion and love for people once they roll up their sleeves and get going.

ONE VOLUNTEER STORY:

The evening before a teen girls' backpacking trip, several of us were still in the office completing our extensive checklist of items we better not forget. There would be no quick run to a grocery store to replace anything we left behind. The phone rang close to quitting time. It was a TYM volunteer extraordinaire, Lisa Sobrato – soon to become Lisa Sonsini. She was within a month of her wedding and wanted to know if we needed any help on the trip. We were actually overstaffed, and I let her know we were okay without her. She responded quickly, "No, I know you don't *need* my help, but I am going kind of crazy around here. *I* need to go."

As I had come to expect from the dozens of camps where Lisa was on volunteer staff, she always operates 100% in the moment. I am not sure any of the teens knew anything about her upcoming wedding plans. But for one of our girls, her presence was indeed God sent.

Lisa was part of a team with several girls, and one in particular had decided she simply would not go to the bathroom in the wilderness under any circumstances. That decision worked for a day or so, but eventually everything fell apart for her. Unable to hold it all in, her clothes became urine and feces soaked. At first, she denied she needed any help.

Lisa knew better. She rigged up a private shower using trees, rope, a plastic tarp and towels, and heated enough water for the task at hand. Twenty minutes later, with Lisa's constant encouragement and help, our camper was clean and ready for the next activity. Not many knew what was going on, definitely appropriate in this situation.

The rest of the trip was filled with laughter and delight, and Lisa left relaxed and ready for her fast-paced schedule toward marriage.

Lisa first volunteered with Today's Youth Matter when – as an attorney – she walked us through the maze of paperwork to obtain our non-profit, tax-exempt status. And for the next twenty years she served as driver, team leader, support staff and camp director for multiple winter and summer programs. As our TYM Board Chair she guided the ministry through sharp growing pains and helped find and secure a more permanent site for our camp use over a sixteen-year period.

The Anatomy Of A Volunteer

After leaving the law firm to pilot her own extended family through the maze of details to establish the Sobrato Family Foundation, Lisa began to mentor a young TYM girl struggling to grow up. A few days after she left the practice of law, Lisa and her young charge took on the task of digging an outhouse hole by hand at our new TYM camp amidst mosquitoes and extreme heat. That memory – one of many – is indelibly carved into their DNA together. Lisa tells me they often bring it up in conversation as a turning point for both of them. Of course, there were literally hundreds of positive – and a few negative – memories, but it once again brings home the reality that investing in the life of another reaps huge rewards no one can quite anticipate if we stick with it over time. Today that young woman, having graduated from college with honors is serving as a clerk for a Santa Clara County DA's office and is now a Legal Secretary in the County. She is planning to attend law school and follow in her mentor's footsteps.

Lisa admitted that on her first snow TYM camp she was a bit intimidated by our girls. She would be the first to tell you, "If I can do it, anyone can."

And so can you!

Forty-four Suggestions to Get You Started

So you want to do something to make a difference in your hometown, in the United States or in the world, but you are not quite sure where to start? There is no doubt that your creativity and common sense will guide you toward some amazing, never-been-done-before, far-reaching ideas and activities. Find your Popeye moment. That moment when you boldly proclaim, "That's all I can stand. I can't stands no more." Look for potholes. Do not limit yourself. The following is simply a partial list of ideas that might help get you started.

Frederick Buechner wrote, "The place God calls you to is the place where your deep gladness and the world's deep hunger meet."[4] Ask yourself, "Where do I find my deep joy? Does the world hunger for it?" Most likely you are one step closer to finding and putting into action that which you alone have been created to fulfill.

It is worth repeating, this is only a very partial list. You have permission and are encouraged to step out in any direction, as God seems to nudge you.

Forty-four Suggestions to Get You Started

1. Decide to dump the excuses. When you are tempted to say, "I am too old, too young, overweight, retired, uninformed, in school, don't drive, too busy or too tired," take a good look at yourself and agree with every serious athlete – NO EXCUSES!
2. Reread Philippians 4 to get an authentic picture of the race we are really running. Remember to fix your eyes on the prize.
3. Check out the Internet for non-profits in your area. Most of them depend heavily on volunteers to keep afloat. Do your homework and make sure their philosophy aligns with your own.
4. Get involved financially. Your generosity – no matter the size of the gift – may make a huge difference. Your support will be genuinely appreciated. If you are not immediately thanked, preferably by a phone call, and a receipt sent within a few days, find a new place for your donations.
5. If you ask yourself, "How much should I give?" a good rule of thumb (according to Jerry Panas of the Institute of Charitable Giving) is to give until you feel proud.
6. Your church undoubtedly has a number of volunteer opportunities. (But remember that helping out with a luncheon or Bible study at church where you are a participant doesn't count. You are just doing your "family" thing.)

7. Every local school in your community has huge needs. Pick a low-performing school. Make the call. You can help a child in math, read your favorite story to a group of children, listen to a child read to you, take on yard duty during recesses or help a teacher cleanup the classroom. You are not necessarily making a lifetime commitment, although it may turn out to be just that. But you have to make the call. You will most likely need to be fingerprinted. It is for the protection of everyone involved.
8. Keep your eyes open. Maybe a child living just a few doors away has a need for a tutor or a friend. Most parents welcome your help. Just make sure to get permission from a parent first.
9. Do not be afraid to ask for help – from your pastor, from a teacher, from a friend or a non-profit.
10. Work with others. Do not forget that even the Lone Ranger had Tonto.
11. Laughter is great medicine. Lavish plenty of humor in whatever you decide to do. Keep a mental diary of Knock-Knock or other G-rated jokes.
12. Remember to take time for yourself. The Bible says to stay "Fueled and aflame." Spending every waking hour pouring into others will leave you drained and hopelessly useless.
13. Make a "priority list." If you were to die tomorrow, would you like to be remembered as that lady with all

her cats, or that guy who was in such terrific shape? Or perhaps you might be remembered as that person who traveled the world (or the country, state, city or neighborhood) finding ways to help others. What would you like to leave as your legacy?

14. Be flexible. Sometimes we go into a situation with expectations of how we want it done only to discover that our way may not be the only way. Be willing to listen to what others want to do, and do not insist on your own way.

15. Become a prayer partner. There are so many good stories in scripture about what persistent prayer and petitioning can do. Keep praying and praying and praying. (There are some excellent books on prayer. They are encouraging and can also serve as a great guide. Visit your church library or find a local Christian bookstore.) Remember that praying is a two-way conversation with God. Make sure you are doing as much listening as you are talking.

16. It is sometimes helpful to keep a number of lists as you move forward. Get several large pieces of paper and tape them to your wall. One might be entitled *Grace Happened Here*. Another you can label *Reasons to Express Gratitude*. Then start filling in the details. You will find hundreds of reasons for gratitude and equally as many to recognize God's grace is all around you.

17. Adopt a child from another country. For under forty dollars a month, you can keep a child fed, dressed and in school. Maybe the money spent on that extra-hot, white chocolate mocha soy latte espresso something-or-other is not as necessary as you thought.
18. If you do "adopt" a child from another country, save up enough money to go to his or her birthplace. Both of you will be better because of the experience.
19. Keep your eyes open in the grocery store. Frazzled mothers with four children under the age of seven are everywhere. Keep a small bottle of bubbles to blow, or a really cool string game. Be prepared to read a book just in case.
20. Invite a homeless person you have usually ignored asking for money on the street corner to join you for lunch. Just make sure it is safe.
21. Go to a park and bring Frisbees, bubbles, hula-hoops and long ropes for group jump rope. Lay them out for kids to use and encourage them to do so. If you have the financial resources, let them take what you brought home with them. Again remember, safety first.
22. Volunteer as a hospice worker for a special needs child. Many parents need a break, and you might just be the answer to their prayers.
23. Take a class at your community college, and get really good at story telling. Then volunteer at a school, the library, even at a local park. Wear a wild hat – maybe

Forty-four Suggestions to Get You Started

purple or red – so children will be able to see and recognize you coming.

24. Make it a family practice to serve a meal at a rescue mission once a month. The mission needs your help, and your children will learn the precious gift of service. Infrequently a rescue mission has more volunteers than needed. Find a new place more fitting for your needs.
25. Drive an elderly person to the doctor's office or grocery store. And remember NOT to become impatient when he moves slowly or wants to show you how to pick out the best pineapple or kumquat in the store.
26. Go to a nursing home. Regularly. Nearly seventy-five percent of people living in nursing homes have no one come and visit at all! Plan to be stretched and touched.
27. Always be prepared to share the Good/Great News. If we depend only upon bona fide pastors with doctorates to bring people to Christ, we will be missing many people that would never, ever walk through a door of a physical church. You become their church experience.
28. Video game rooms are everywhere in movie theaters and shopping malls. If you are really good at a particular game and can play forever on one slim quarter, play for a while and then pass the game off to a beginner. Smile and wink when they type in their initials at getting a really high score.

29. Take time to listen. At church. At home. In the park. On your commute bus or train. Wherever you are. The world needs many more listeners.
30. Introduce young people to new experiences. Perhaps it is your love of classical music. Play a game of kick-the-can – if you are old enough to remember how to play kick-the-can!
31. Teach some children the dance of your teen years. The Charleston, the Twist, the Funky Chicken, Thriller. Let them see you are not afraid to look silly.
32. Volunteer to coach some children (not your own) in a sport you love. Then sign them up in a local league. Many vulnerable children dream of the day they will be drafted by the NBA or the NFL. But they have to get started somewhere!
33. Volunteer to serve at a day or overnight camp. Clean bathrooms. Prepare meals. Take on a job that maybe isn't too glamorous but is essential for the success of the camp experience.
34. Join a church short-term mission trip. You will receive considerably more than you can possibly give. That's the miracle of service. Do not back out with the excuse that mission trips are only for young people.
35. Encourage your church to move one Sunday service into the street. What would happen in your community if an entire congregation decided to spend a Sunday fixing up a school, painting the home of a very low income

resident, doing yard work, visiting a few nursing homes or cleaning up a local park? Then gather together in the evening to share your successes – and yes, maybe less than perfect experiences. The Word going into the street is powerful indeed.

36. Invite that new person walking into your church to sit with you. Then follow up with lunch, even if they are not dressed just like you.

37. Keep your eyes open for opportunities to serve. You'll be changed from the inside out.

38. God created you to do His work. Remember, if you don't do *you*, *you* simply will not get done.

39. Carry a menagerie of finger puppets in your purse or pocket. Since there are no moving parts, anyone can make them work. All you have to do is wiggle your fingers. You can have a portable puppet theater wherever you go. (It also helps to practice just a little in front of a mirror.)

40. Decide each day to seek out a person in need. Keep your eyes open. It could be in a grocery store, on your street, in your apartment building, on a local playground or on the train to work.

41. Become environmentally sensitive. Remember, this is God's earth. It is our job to take the best care of it that we possibly can. Join a beach or park or school cleanup day. Decide to take a leadership role for the day – and don't forget to take lots of pictures.

42. Organize a neighborhood block party. Get the police to agree to block off the street. Everyone bring some food. Make sure that anyone playing a musical instrument – professionally or strictly amateur – brings it out for the occasion.
43. Go to a local hardware store and buy half-inch PVC pipe cut into two-foot lengths. You will need eight to twelve of them. Buy a bag of mini-marshmallows. During your block party – or at a local park or playground – pass out the PVC pipe and a sandwich bag filled with the mini-marshmallows. They make great "shooters" and no one gets hurt when shot with a marshmallow. Just remember to clean up after the game.
44. Stick with it. If you start working with a vulnerable child, it takes about fifty memories for that child to begin to even think about trusting you. There is actually no reason for a young person (or a vulnerable adult) who has already experienced years of abuse and neglect to take one look at you and decide you are indeed any different from all the other adults in his or her life. Be patient. Decide that you will not quit easily; that you are in it for the long haul. It takes lots and lots time to build fifty memories.

A Final Note

First Corinthians Chapter 13 is aptly named "The Love Chapter," and it concludes with wise words for all of us. Eugene Peterson's The Message translates it: Trust steadily in God. Hope unswervingly. Love extravagantly.

> **Trust Steadily in God.** That comes first. I have been privileged to work with vulnerable children in a camp setting for many years, and sometimes when I am standing in the midst of total, unrestrained, unbelievable chaos, this is a very good thing to remember. You and I are stuck in the circumstances surrounding us. God can see the whole picture, the only view that counts.
>
> **Hope Unswervingly.** In his masterful book The Hope Quotient, Ray Johnson reminds us hope is the one ingredient that can turn an upside down life, right side up. That is very evident with our TYM children. Hope is only a distant dream

for the eight year old who lost both parents in one brutal, ugly evening, when he witnessed his father in a fit of uncontrollable rage kill his mother and shortly afterwards disappear in handcuffs on his way to a life sentence in prison. He will have a painfully slow healing process, but without hope, he has no chance whatsoever.

Love extravagantly. We've all been to that potluck where at one end of the table sits the most mouth-watering, delicious lasagna devoured within minutes and at the other end that still untouched bowl of Jell-O with a cut up banana in it. It takes time to express extravagant love. One of my favorite extravagant love stories tells of an elderly woman walking through a park with her picnic basket. She comes across a young homeless man beginning to eat his dry-crusted, made who knows when peanut butter sandwich. She politely suggests they pool their resources and eat together. He agrees and she carefully spreads out the tablecloth and covers it with her famous fried chicken, veggies with homemade humus, freshly squeezed orange juice, potato salad and still warm apple pie. Then she takes his sandwich and carefully cuts it into four pieces and lays it on one of her

China plates. And the first thing she eats after blessing the food? You guessed it. His peanut butter sandwich! That's extravagant love!

ENDNOTES

1. Ryan Shafer, P.E., G.E. Principal
2. The Pursuit of Wow by Tom Peters, page 228 A Vintage Original, First Edition copyright 1994,
3. National Juvenile Justice Network How to Calculate the Cost of Youth Arrest August 2013 (www.njjn.org)
4. Wishful Thinking: A Theological ABC by Frederick Buechner